REFLECTIONS ON 30 YEARS OF THE ASIAN DEVELOPMENT BANK ADMINISTRATIVE TRIBUNAL

DECEMBER 2021

ASIAN DEVELOPMENT BANK

ADB

Contents

Message from Judge Shin-ichi Ago
President of the ADB Administrative Tribunal

First of all, I would like to extend my deepest condolences to the families, friends, and colleagues of those who succumbed to COVID-19, while remaining deeply concerned that a huge number of people remain at risk. I would also like to pay highest respect to the huge number of medical professionals who are dedicated to life-saving activities. Originally, this welcome greeting would have been given verbally in front of many participants on the first day of a face-to-face conference. However, the pandemic, which has been rampant since early 2020, made it impossible to do so. Under these circumstances, this preface to the memorial collection of essays is being offered instead of an opening address.

We at the Asian Development Bank Administrative Tribunal (ADBAT) are delighted that the Tribunal is celebrating its 30th anniversary, and I am privileged and honored to write this preface in my capacity as its current President. Although our Tribunal is not as large as some other tribunals, the fact that we have handed down more than 120 decisions in the last 30 years can be evaluated as a decent performance in its own way. Keeping pace with legal and practical developments, the Tribunal also recently revised its rules. For detailed information on the 30-year history of the Tribunal, please refer to the contribution in this book prepared by the Senior Attorney to the Tribunal, who has served the Tribunal longer than anyone else.

Considering the fact that the judicial institutions, which are called international administrative tribunals, represent a relatively new entity in the international community (the International Labour Organization Administrative Tribunal, which has been active for the longest time among all of its peers, has not yet reached its century mark), 30 years can fairly be said as a milestone. As an intergovernmental organization, the Asian Development Bank (ADB) enjoys certain privileges and immunities. This means that the judicial power of the countries in which it operates does not automatically extend to the resolution of issues involving employment relationships within the organization. International administrative tribunals inevitably emerged from that particular situation so as to provide an avenue of redress consonant with the right to a fair and impartial tribunal as provided under Article 10 of the Universal Declaration of Human Rights. Tribunals thus established to provide judicial remedies for the staff working in intergovernmental institutions that enjoy privileges and immunities had to pioneer an unknown field of law, which is neither national nor international. For these tribunals are detached from the national jurisdiction of the host state, but at the same time, unlike the International Court of Justice, the International Criminal Court, or the European Court of Human Rights, they are not established by international treaties. They are usually set up by decisions of the principal governance organs of the institutions concerned. However, these tribunals are not subsidiary organs of the institutions, and they enjoy independent status. This peculiar nature of international administrative tribunals makes their legal position somewhat unclear. It is not obvious what kind of law is actually applied and by what criteria a judgment is rendered in these peculiar judicial institutions. I have developed my thoughts about this special status of international administrative tribunals, to be published separately but in conjunction with this book, as explained further below. The various legal rules, including tribunal procedures, applied in examining claims are an outcome of an accumulation of factual practices. Activities of an international administrative tribunal can, therefore, be analogous to voyages into uncharted waters, equivalent to a similar situation where many international legal rules customarily arise from the repetition of mere practices.

The number of administrative tribunals related to various intergovernmental organizations has increased rather recently and rapidly. Furthermore, it has now become a practice for each of them to invite judges and registrars of other tribunals to their commemorative events every 10 years or so. Judges serving on international administrative tribunals can exchange experiences in person at such conferences. This year, in fact, our 30th anniversary event coincides with that of the Inter-American Bank Administrative Tribunal, and if COVID-19 had not prevailed, many of the participants would have had to travel long distances to attend similar activities two times in a row. That kind of conference, held to celebrate the establishment of those tribunals, can play an important role. For there are many things to learn from other tribunals, and the pool of knowledge and experience is a huge asset for those involved in international adjudication processes.

Since each tribunal is independent of each other, there is no need to create a common case law. Harmonization among procedural rules is also not required. However, each judicial institution, which is neither a national court of law nor an international court applying established rules of international law, does produce a sort of legal precedent with a certain tendency to converge with one another. This is reflected in the mutual citation of judgments. We find many instances in judgments of various tribunals where the notion of international administrative law is employed. If something exists that is frequently referred to as "international administrative law" (or, in my view, better termed "law of international civil servants"), it can only be inductively drawn from the experiences of other institutions. In that sense, it is regrettable that the ADBAT commemorative conference cannot be held face-to-face. Personal contacts and exchanges of opinions by judges, taking place sometimes off the record in the corridor, may provide useful ideas to improve the operation of an international administrative tribunal.

In the current abnormal situation, many tribunals have been working remotely. This Tribunal also held a full-scale remote session last year for the first time in its history. And today, instead of a face-to-face commemorative conference, we are celebrating our 30th anniversary by publishing a book. Contributions by two of the past presiding judges of the Tribunal, the chair of the ADB Staff Association and a representative of the General Counsel's Office, the Tribunal's Senior Attorney (with her account of the 30-year history), the Tribunal's Legal Assistant (with an indexed table of tediously compiled key words), and the Executive Secretary of the Tribunal assisted by a competent Tribunal Assistant (with an interesting sketch of the performance statistics), together comprise the contents of this commemorative publication.

Normally, contributions by the five judges, including myself, who currently serve on the Tribunal would be found as well in the commemorative volume, but this time, we adopted a different method. The *Asian Journal of International Law*, a periodical published by the Asian Society of International Law, agreed to celebrate the ADBAT's anniversary by devoting a section to the ADBAT. Therefore, we decided to place the contributions of active judges in this journal, thereby trying to create a synergy effect involving the ADBAT, academia, and legal practitioners. This book should thus be read together with the forthcoming issue of the *Asian Journal of International Law* in its special memorial section on the ADBAT. Given the fact that administrative tribunals are hybrid in nature or *sui generis* creatures, and that the anniversary event is being held in an equally hybrid manner, I am certain that this hybrid publication will be both symbolic and meaningful. I hope you will join us in celebrating the ADBAT's 30th anniversary by reading and enjoying this publication in conjunction with that of the academic journal.

Message from Judge Arnold Zack

Former President of the ADB Administrative Tribunal

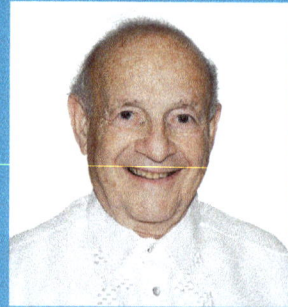

As a former ADBAT Judge, I offer my heartiest congratulations to the ADB Administrative Tribunal for 30 years of service to ADB and its staff.

Ten years ago, I was honored to be President of the Administrative Tribunal when we celebrated the 20th anniversary of the creation of the ADBAT by convening a meeting of judges and international experts from other administrative tribunals at ADB's Manila headquarters on 5 September 2011. Our goal was to exchange ideas about procedures best calculated to protect and enhance the balance between rapid resolution of staff complaints and litigation before administrative tribunals as the final adjudicators. We opted to focus on how the earlier steps in that dispute resolution procedure can be best structured to ensure that most of the disputes are readily resolved as soon as possible after they emerge, while further encouraging such resolution as an alternative to tribunal determinations.

Although individual administrative tribunals may differ in their approaches, we sought to emphasize the importance of assuring staff that the procedures used are fair and fairly administered, and that resorting to the organization's tribunal provides a full opportunity to present the positions of the staff member and employer or a resolution that is consistent with the laws of the organization and the standards of due process expected of all international tribunals.

The papers presented at that session were published and hopefully helped other tribunals to strengthen the efficiency of their procedures.

This year, as we emerge from the year of isolation due to the pandemic, we are deprived of the camaraderie and opportunity for informal exchange of ideas and experiences in our global effort to provide more equitable procedures for resolving workplace disputes. But ADB is to be commended for its effort this year to perpetuate the tradition of idea exchange in this "distance" format. Hopefully, we will soon be able to return to the more informal and usually very productive format of in-person intellectual exchange.

Again, my best wishes to all those within ADB and its Administrative Tribunal as you continue your effort toward early and just resolution of workplace disputes within ADB, consistent with its commitment to upholding the Rule of Law.

It gives me great pleasure to write this message, in the special publication being brought out on the 30th anniversary of the establishment of the Asian Development Bank Administrative Tribunal (ADBAT). I recall that 10 years ago, the ADBAT had completed 20 years, and I had just joined the Tribunal. In those 10 years, I have seen the work of this Tribunal, in the beginning as a member, and later as the President of the Tribunal as of February 2014. The cordiality that has marked the Tribunal's proceedings has stood out as one of the outstanding characteristics of the working of the Tribunal. During the period that I have been associated with the Tribunal, from February 2010 to January 2019, there was not one dissenting judgment out of the nearly 30 judgments delivered by the Tribunal.

The cordiality was not restricted to the members and staff of the Tribunal, but also pervaded the conduct of the aggrieved staff and the top executives of the bank.

The President of the bank traditionally hosted a formal lunch for the members of the Tribunal and the Executive Secretary, along with some senior officers of the bank, including the Representative of the Staff Council, the Ombudsman, the General Counsel, and the Chairperson of the Appeals Committee. Of course, we never touched upon any particular case, but we were informed about the recent highlights of the bank's activities in various spheres in many countries.

In the earlier years, we often referred to past decisions of the International Labour Organization Administrative Tribunal (ILOAT), the World Bank Administrative Tribunal (WBAT), and other international administrative tribunals' decisions, as precedents. In the later years, we took pride in referring to the precedents from our own earlier decided cases of the ADBAT.

We have had interesting meetings from time to time with the Committee of Administrative Tribunal Matters, in which we had some useful feedback from the staff of the bank, for example, on the language of the judgments and some remedies that had caused them concern. The clarifications provided convinced them, all the more, that the Tribunal works as an independent judicial body, considers the full interests of the aggrieved staff member, and that all of the submissions of the parties were in accordance with the relevant law and judicial principles. This gave us a feeling that the aggrieved Applicant trusted the Tribunal to in fact deliver due justice in a case. In other words, the Tribunal has always attempted to provide adequate remedies to the parties to a case, within the framework of the provisions of the ADBAT Statute, 1991, and the Rules of Procedure.

While the members of the Tribunal came from different countries and systems of law and jurisprudence, and brought their own expertise to the specific issues of a particular case, they soon converged in a unanimous decision after several rounds of incisive discussions, which was very satisfying.

I also send best wishes to ADBAT President, Judge Shin-ichi Ago and his team for bringing out a special publication on the occasion of the 30th anniversary of the ADBAT.

In these days of the COVID-19 pandemic, we are denied the opportunity to meet in person, in Manila, the other members of the Tribunal, as well as the specialists and experts from other international administrative tribunals, as was the practice earlier.

I want to conclude this message by affirming that we will all meet in some part of the world from time to time, stretching out our hands of cordiality, and sharing the expertise we have gathered in strengthening the international administrative law principles and jurisprudence.

Reflections on the 30 Years of Operation of the ADB Administrative Tribunal

Profiles of the Incumbent Members and Secretariat of the ADB Administrative Tribunal

Shin-ichi Ago, President

Judge Ago, a national of Japan, was appointed as a member to the Administrative Tribunal in 2013. He is a professor at the Ritsumeikan University and director of the Kyoto Museum for World Peace. He is also a professor emeritus, former law dean, and vice-president at Kyushu University. He is a member of the International Labour Organization Committee of Experts on the Application of Conventions and Recommendations.

Anne Trebilcock, Vice-President

Judge Trebilcock, a national of the United States, was appointed as a member to the Administrative Tribunal in 2015. She is the vice-president of the GAVI Alliance Appeals Tribunal and an on-call arbitrator of the International Development Law Organization. She is a former legal adviser of the International Labour Organization and is associated with the Labour Law Institute of Georg-August University in Göttingen.

Chris de Cooker, Member

Judge de Cooker, a national of the Netherlands, was appointed as a member to the Administrative Tribunal in 2015. He is the current president of the North Atlantic Treaty Organization Administrative Tribunal and a member of the European Bank for Reconstruction and Development Administrative Tribunal. He is a judge of the Organisation for Economic Co-operation and Development Administrative Tribunal and GAVI Appeals Tribunal. He was the chairman of the Global Fund Appeal Board as well as the Appeal Board of the International Bureau of Weights and Measures. He is a mediator at the ITER Organization and author of various legal publications and reports.

Raul Pangalangan, Member

Judge Pangalangan, a national of the Philippines, was appointed as member to the Administrative Tribunal in 2019. He served as judge in the International Criminal Court. He is a professor of law and former law dean of the University of the Philippines. He has held visiting appointments or lectureships, *inter alia*, at Harvard Law School, The Hague Academy of International Law, and Salzburg Seminar on International Criminal Law. He is a *membre associé* in the Institut de Droit International, a member of the Permanent Court of Arbitration, and part of the executive council of Asian Society of International Law.

Silvia Cartwright, Member

Judge Cartwright, a national of New Zealand, was appointed as member to the Administrative Tribunal in 2020. She is a member of the Executive Committee of International Commission of Jurists. She served as governor-general of New Zealand from 2001 to 2006. She is a former chief judge of the District Courts and judge of the High Court of New Zealand. She was also a judge in the Trial Chamber of the Extraordinary Chambers in the Courts of Cambodia. She is a fellow at the Hastings Institute.

Cesar L. Villanueva, Executive Secretary

Cesar Villanueva, from the Philippines, was appointed as Executive Secretary of the Administrative Tribunal in 2011. He is the founding Partner of Villanueva Gabionza & Dy law firm. He was the former Chairman of the Governance Commission for Government-Owned-or-Controlled Corporations (GCG). He is a professor and former dean of the Ateneo de Manila Law School. He served as Chairman of the Commercial Law Department of the Philippine Judicial Academy of the Supreme Court and was a member of the Governing Board of the Mandatory Continuing Legal Education. He is an author of legal books and articles, mainly on corporate law and governance, and commercial law.

Christine Griffiths, Senior Attorney to the Administrative Tribunal

Christine Griffiths, from Australia, was appointed to the Administrative Tribunal in 2003. Prior to joining ADB, she spent several years in practice as a commercial litigation lawyer with Gadens Ridgeway Solicitors and as a lawyer advising the Australian government on international law issues.

Filemon Ray Javier, Legal Assistant

Filemon Ray Javier, from the Philippines, was appointed to the Administrative Tribunal in 2019. He is a Founding Partner at Tolosa Javier Lim & Chua Law Firm, in which he focuses on labor, civil, and criminal litigation. He is also a professor of law and a Philippine bar examination reviewer in labor and employment laws.

Michael Julius Rubio, Senior Tribunal Operations Assistant

Michael Julius Rubio joined ADB in 2014 as Administrative Assistant for the Staff Council. He was then transferred to the Office of The Secretary in 2016 and worked with the Administrative Tribunal. He has a master's degree in public administration and holds a bachelor's degree in communication.

The ADB Administrative Tribunal during a virtual session held in October 2020 (photo by M. J. Rubio).

Profiles of the Past Presidents
of the ADB Administrative Tribunal

Elihu Lauterpacht (United Kingdom)

October 1991–July 1995

Professor Sir Lauterpacht was one of the members of the Administrative Tribunal after it was established in 1991 and its first chairman until 1995. He was a judge in the International Court of Justice and other international jurisdictions and English courts. He became the president of the East African Market Tribunal and a member of the Panel of the United Nations Compensation Commission, the World Bank Administrative Tribunal, and the Eritrea-Ethiopia Boundary Commission. He was a lecturer at the Hague Academy of International Law and was a member of the Institut de Droit International.

Source: University of Cambridge. Lauterpacht Centre for International Law. https://www.lcil.cam. ac.uk/about-centrehistory/professor-sir-elihu-lauterpacht.

Florentino P. Feliciano (Philippines)

October 1991–July 1995
October 2006–September 2009

Justice Feliciano was one of the members of the Administrative Tribunal after it was established in 1991, and later served as its president from 2007 to 2009. He was an associate justice of the Supreme Court of the Philippines. He served as Chairman of the Appellate Body of the World Trade Organization in Geneva. He was appointed as a member of the World Bank Administrative Tribunal. He served as a member of different international panels of arbitrators, including the International Chamber of Commerce, International Court of Arbitration. He was a professorial lecturer in law at the University of the Philippines and a lecturer at the Hague Academy of International Law. He served as legal consultant in the Consultative Committee on Establishment of the Asian Development Bank; United Nations Economic

Commission for Asia and the Far East; and Preparatory Committee on the Asian Development Bank.

Source: United Nations Audiovisual Library of International Law. https://legal.un.org/avl/pdf/ls/Feliciano_bio.pdf.

Mark H. Fernando (Sri Lanka)

October 1991–September 2002

Judge Fernando was one of the members of the Administrative Tribunal after it was established in 1991, and later served as its president from 1996 to 2002. He was appointed as judge in the Supreme Court of Sri Lanka. He served as judge in the Administrative Tribunal of the International Labour Organization. He was posthumously conferred a "Special Award of Excellence for a Lifetime of Integrity" by Transparency International, Sri Lanka.

Source: C. Mendis. 2011. TISL Honours Justice Mark Fernando for 'Lifetime of Integrity.' *Daily FT*. 10 December. https://www.ft.lk/article/59958/TISL-honours-Justice-Mark-Fernando-for--Lifetime-of-Integrity-.

Robert A. Gorman (United States)

August 1995–July 2004

Professor Gorman was the president of the Administrative Tribunal from 2003 to 2004. He served as president and vice-president of the World Bank Administrative Tribunal and president of the Inter-American Development Bank Administrative Tribunal. He was part of the American Arbitration Association, Labor-Arbitration Panel. He became president of the American Association of University Professors and the Association of American Law Schools. He is a Kenneth W. Gemmill professor emeritus at the University of Pennsylvania Carey Law School. He was also a visiting professor at Harvard Law School, New York University, and the University of Southern California.

Source: Penn Law. University of Pennsylvania Carey Law School. https://www.law.upenn.edu/faculty/ragorman/.

Flerida Ruth P. Romero (Philippines)

October 2001–September 2006

Justice Romero was the president of the Administrative Tribunal from 2005 to 2006. She was an associate justice in the Supreme Court of the Philippines. She served as special assistant to the President of the Philippines. She headed the Philippine delegation to the International Women's Year Conference in Mexico in 1975. She served as president of the Philippine Women Judges Association, as international director of the International Association of Women Judges, and as consultant to the University of the Philippines Women Lawyer's Circle. She became the director and dean of the University of the Philippines School of Labor and Industrial Relations.

Sources: Republic of the Philippines, Senate Electoral Tribunal. https://www.set.gov.ph/member-justices/1275/hon-justice-flerida-ruth-p-romero/; Indiana University, Maurer School of Law. https://www.repository.law.indiana.edu/notablealumni/12/.

Arnold M. Zack (United States)

August 2004–July 2013

Professor Zack was the president of the Administrative Tribunal from 2010 to 2013. He is a senior research associate at the Harvard Law School. He was the former president of the National Academy of Arbitrators. He became a member of the Steering Committee for the Permanent Court of Arbitration in the Hague. He served as a consultant for the governments of the United States (Department of State, Peace Corps, Department of Labor, Department of Commerce), Australia, Cambodia, Greece, Israel, Italy, the Philippines, and South Africa, as well as for the International Labour Organization, International Monetary Fund, Inter-American Development Bank, and United Nations Development Programme. He is an author of numerous books on labor mediation and arbitration.

Source: Harvard University. Labor and Worklife Program, A Program of the Harvard Law School. https://lwp.law.harvard.edu/people/arnold-zack.

Lakshmi Swaminathan (India)

February 2010–January 2019

Judge Swaminathan was the president of the Administrative Tribunal from 2014 to 2019. She retired as vice-chairman (Judicial) of the Principal Bench at New Delhi of the Central Administrative Tribunal, which is equivalent to the status of a High Court Judge. She served as Joint Secretary and Legal Advisor in the Ministry of Law and Justice of India. She was the vice-chairman and principal advisor of the Waterfalls Institute of Technology Transfer in New Delhi. She was an arbitrator for the National Stock Exchange of India, Ltd. and in Adjudication of Disputes between Central Government Departments and private parties and public sector undertakings. She was a member of the Indian Council of Arbitrators and panels of arbitrators and mediators of the Governing Council of the International Centre for Alternate Dispute Resolution.

Gillian Triggs (Australia)

October 2012–August 2019

Professor Triggs was the president of the Administrative Tribunal in 2019. She is currently the Assistant Secretary-General serving as the Assistant High Commissioner for Protection of the Office of the United Nations High Commissioner for Refugees. She served as president of the Australian Human Rights Commission. She was a vice-chancellor's fellow, a director, and a professor of law at the University of Melbourne. She became the dean, a challis professor on international law, and professor emeritus at the University of Sydney. She was the chair of the Board of Justice Connect, and director of Melbourne University Publishing. She served as director of the British Institute of International and Comparative Law. She was a member of the International Academy of Comparative Law and Australian Academy of Law.

Celebrating the Tribunal's 30-Year Anniversary through a Reflection on Key Decisions

Damien Eastman, Assistant General Counsel
Office of the General Counsel, ADB

"There is therefore a vacuum which needs to be filled by the organizations themselves. The creation of an independent body, empowered to make binding decisions in legal disputes between an organization and its staff, is by no means an altruistic gesture from the organization's point of view; without it, officials might suffer from a sense of injustice which would impair the smooth running of the Secretariat."[1]

Since its establishment in 1991 as an independent judicial body, composed of members who are preeminent jurists, the Asian Development Bank (ADB) Administrative Tribunal (the Tribunal) has played a fundamental role in ensuring that issues and disputes between ADB and its staff are addressed fairly and transparently. This has supported ADB in achieving its goal of a prosperous, inclusive, resilient, and sustainable Asia and the Pacific.

Having issued 125 decisions[2] over the course of 30 years, the Tribunal's decisions have helped shape ADB employment policies, procedures, and actions. Accordingly, in celebrating the Tribunal's 30th anniversary, a number of the Tribunal's decisions deserve to be highlighted, as they demonstrate the clear contribution that the Tribunal has made to ADB and to ensuring transparency and accountability in ADB staff matters.

These selected decisions address three key areas: (i) applicable law, (ii) the terms and conditions of appointment ("fundamental and essential" terms or acquired rights), and (iii) the Tribunal's own jurisdictional limits. These rulings have provided both ADB and its staff with essential and clear guidance and support in managing staff matters.

The Body of Law, Principles, and Policies Governing Staff Employment

When considering matters relating to staff employment, it is important to first determine the body of law, principles, and policies that govern the terms and

---

[1] M.B. Akehurst. 1967. *The Law Governing Employment in International Organizations*. Cambridge: University Press. p. 12.

[2] As of 15 July 2021.

conditions of ADB staff employment. In its inaugural decision in *Lindsey v. ADB* in 1992,[3] the Tribunal set out the ADB staff employment framework to comprise

- the constituent instruments of the bank,
- general principles of law,
- the contract between ADB and its staff member,
- the Staff Rules and Regulations,
- administrative orders and circulars, and
- the decisions of international administrative tribunals when dealing with comparable situations.

While broad and all-encompassing, the Tribunal also set out that this framework remains subject to the recognition and protection of any fundamental and essential terms of employment of the staff member.

This initial framing of the body of rules applicable to staff has provided ADB with a clear architecture to apply to its policies and decisions. ADB management has consistently reflected on this framework and the principles enunciated by the Tribunal in the application of this framework to individual cases when making decisions or applying policies to staff matters. By framing the terms of employment at the outset, the Tribunal ensured that its decisions since have been based on a transparent and accountable footing for both staff and ADB.

Embedding Protection and Developing Understanding of Fundamental and Essential Terms of Employment

Throughout its history, ADB has periodically revised the policies and procedures applicable to its staff, factoring in the evolving needs of the institution.

Central to its analysis when amending staff policies and procedures has been an assessment of whether such changes impact a "fundamental and essential" term of employment (also referred to as acquired rights)—that is, a right that is so fundamental and essential to the contractual bargain/agreement between the organization and its staff that it cannot be altered without the staff member's consent.

The Tribunal, in *Mesch and Siy v. ADB* (No. 4) (1997), drew on, and incorporated into its decision, the reasoning applied by other international administrative tribunals, the International Labour Organization Administrative Tribunal (ILOAT) and the World Bank Administrative Tribunal (WBAT), when

---

[3] *Carl Gene Lindsey v. Asian Development Bank, Decision No. 1.* [1992]. 1 ADBAT Reports p. 2.

determining whether an amendment alters an acquired right or a fundamental and essential term.[4]

More recently, the Tribunal, in its decision in *Perrin et al. v. ADB* (No. 3) (2018), restated and built on its earlier statements on the fundamental and essential terms of employment, noting that ADB's authority to amend staff rules is not without limitation and that any amendment must respect both the essential and acquired rights of staff and be reasonable.[5]

While there can be differences of view as to whether a particular change or revision to, for example, a staff benefit program touches on a fundamental and essential term, these Tribunal decisions have provided ADB management with an analytical framework that sets out clear reference points and guidance to (i) assess and determine the scope of its authority to revise the terms and conditions of staff employment, and (ii) ensure that ADB has remained accountable to staff for observing and making decisions that are consistent with these rights.

Exhaustion of Internal Remedies and Adherence with Time Limits

Finally, enabling ADB's internal justice system to function fairly, consistently, and transparently for all parties, the Tribunal has reinforced its jurisdictional limitations where (i) all other remedies available within ADB have not been exhausted (often referred to as "internal remedies"), or (ii) applications to challenge a particular administrative decision are [filed] out of time.[6]

At present, ADB's internal justice system includes a general requirement that staff proceed through a series of steps before a grievance reaches the Tribunal.[7] These "steps below" the Tribunal are the internal remedies referred to in the Tribunal Statute.

---

[4]   In *Ferdinand Mesch and Robert Siy v. Asian Development Bank, No. 4. Decision No. 35.* [1997]. 3 ADBAT Reports "80," "81," the Tribunal, quoting from ILOAT Judgment No. 391 (1980) and WBAT judgment outlined: First, a right should be considered to be acquired when it is laid down in a provision of the Staff Regulations or Staff Rules and is of decisive importance to a candidate for appointment. Alternatively, a right will be acquired if it arises under an express provision of an official contract of appointment and both parties intend that it should be inviolate...it is also possible that a new term which is later incorporated into the contract or staff regulations may become a fundamental and essential term, provided the above conditions are satisfied.

[5]   *Perrin et al. v. Asian Development Bank, No. 3. Decision No. 113.* [2018]. 10 ADBAT Reports "201," "202."

[6]   ADBAT Statute, Article II, Section 3(a) provides for the requirement to exhaust all other remedies available within the bank before a matter is received by the Tribunal. Article II, Section 3(b) specifies the applicable time limits.

[7]   There is a small category of administrative decisions where these requirements do not apply, for example, where the Applicant and the ADB President agree to direct submission of the dispute to the Tribunal; decisions under the Staff Retirement Plan, where a decision of the Administration Committee may be appealed directly to the Tribunal; and decisions concerning the imposition of disciplinary measures, which may be submitted directly for peer review in the Appeals Committee before being eligible for appeal in the Tribunal.

On the need to exhaust internal remedies, in the *Alcartado v. ADB* (1998) ruling, the Tribunal provided some explanation of why the exhaustion of these internal remedies is necessary, and important, before a grievance reaches the Tribunal (which is the final step in ADB's internal justice system):

> "Prompt exhaustion of remedies provides an early opportunity to the institution to rectify possible errors — when memories are fresh, documents are likely to be in hand, and disputed decisions are more amenable to adjustment. This purpose would be significantly undermined if the Tribunal were to condone long and inexcusable delays in the invocation of these remedies ....."[8]

The requirement to exhaust internal remedies is an important feature of ADB's internal justice system. Although some may see these "steps below" the Tribunal as a requirement that adds to the administrative complexity and/or time burden for the grievant, these steps have provided ADB and its staff with the opportunity to fully assess issues and matters internally, undertake further factual investigations where necessary, and for all parties to have before them a full and complete record so as to assist in the determination of whether corrective measures can be applied and are appropriate. This process is effective in practice. It can lead to ADB management taking the appropriate steps to correct an earlier decision should there be a need to do so. It can also assist a grievant to better understand the basis and reasons for management's action/decision.

The legal framework supporting ADB's internal justice system (principally, the relevant ADB Administrative Order and the Tribunal Statute) establishes time frames within which applications must be commenced. On the need to observe these time limits when pursuing a grievance, in the *Behuria v. ADB* (1995) ruling, the Tribunal stated:

> "It is an established principle that in order to fulfill the requirement of exhausting all other remedies available within an organization... it is not sufficient merely to submit a grievance or an appeal to the internal appeal bodies. Such grievance or appeal must be submitted also in conformity with prescribed time-limits."[9]

In the *Alcartado v. ADB* (1998) ruling, the Tribunal touched on the importance of bringing a grievance within the prescribed time frames, stating: *"memories are fresh," "documents are likely to be in hand,"* and *"disputed decisions are more amenable to adjustment."* As a matter of public policy, almost all national legal systems have time limitations in place that preclude the commencement of a legal claim beyond a certain time from the occurrence of an event. Upholding and enforcing these time limits is an important feature of any legal system in balancing the legal rights and interests of all involved. By affirming and upholding the importance of time limits within ADB's internal justice system, the Tribunal

---

[8]   *Roman A. Alcartado v. Asian Development Bank, Decision No. 41.* [1998]. 4 ADBAT Reports p. 72.
[9]   *Sutanu Behuria v. Asian Development Bank, Decision No. 8.* [1995]. 1 ADBAT Reports p. 96.

has provided both staff and ADB with clear guidance and certainty on the time frames to be observed when pursuing and defending staff grievances in ADB's internal justice system.

Concluding Observations

Over the last 30 years, the Tribunal has promoted transparency and accountability in ADB through its rich body of decisions, which are published and available on the Tribunal's publicly accessible website. These decisions have clearly set out the framework and principles that both ADB and its staff continue to refer to when considering their rights, obligations, and limitations. Whether it is through its clear discussion of the body of law applicable to staff matters, terms of appointment, or consistent application of jurisdictional limits, the Tribunal has established itself as an independent judicial entity that has materially enhanced and safeguarded transparency in ADB's internal justice system.

Accordingly, it is with admiration that ADB can look upon the contributions made by the Tribunal over the last 30 years to the organization and its management of staff matters. The Tribunal is to be commended for these contributions on the occasion of its 30th anniversary, and the institution can look forward to the Tribunal's continuing contribution to ADB and its staff over the next 30 years and beyond.

Note: The author wishes to acknowledge the assistance of Nastassja Jardim, Counsel, Office of the General Counsel, in preparing these reflections.

Moving Forward, Looking Back—Strengthening the Internal Justice System

Au Shion Yee, Chairperson, ADB Staff Council

The Staff Council and staff of the Asian Development Bank (ADB) congratulate the ADB Administrative Tribunal (the Tribunal) and its past and present members upon the completion of the milestone of 30 years of providing independent and impartial determinations on the final appeals of staff with respect to their employment disputes. There is an expectation for this to continue for the next 30 years and beyond.

At present there are no cases before the Tribunal. This may indicate that the informal part of the internal justice system that deals with resolving staff grievances and complaints before they reach the highest level of last resort is working well.[10] Equally, however, it could also be reflective of the difficulty staff face in navigating the informal parts of the system. One cannot say without there being more detailed examination of the matter. However, with only 2% or 2 out of the 125 cases that have come before the Tribunal being decided in favor of the Applicant, the Staff Council does share a level of concern and disappointment regarding these results, but concedes that the dynamics and nature of each case are different, and it is difficult to generalize about the efficacy and fairness of the internal justice system based on these statistics alone.

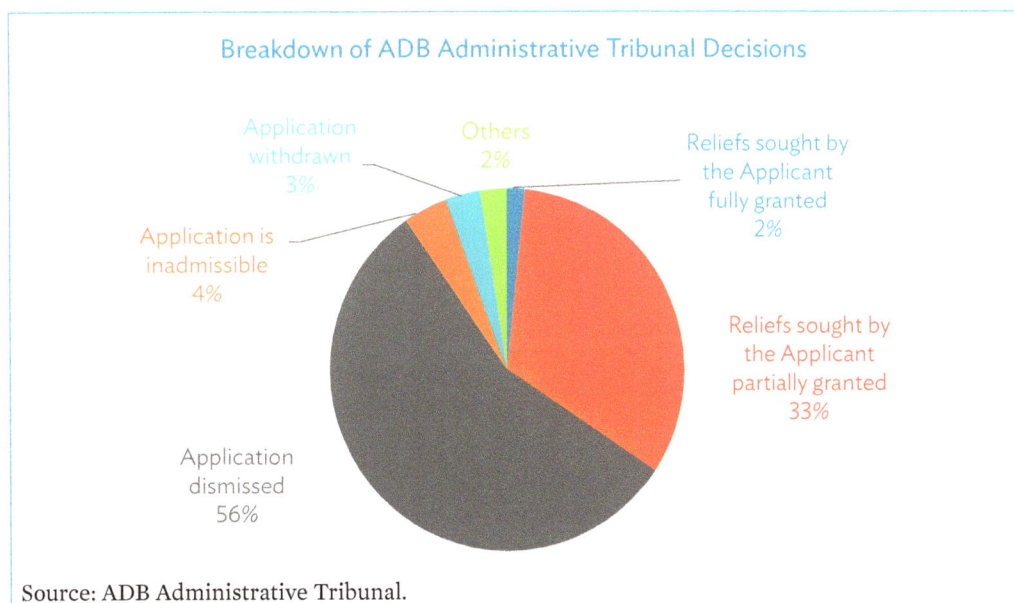

Breakdown of ADB Administrative Tribunal Decisions

- Application withdrawn 3%
- Others 2%
- Reliefs sought by the Applicant fully granted 2%
- Application is inadmissible 4%
- Reliefs sought by the Applicant partially granted 33%
- Application dismissed 56%

Source: ADB Administrative Tribunal.

---

[10] The informal part of the internal justice system refers to all the internal processes and procedures for grievance and conflict resolution leading up to, but excluding, the level of the ADB Administrative Tribunal.

While the final level of appeal of dispute resolution is fully functional and dispenses justice fairly and independently, it is the view of the Staff Council that there are serious issues within the lower parts of the internal dispute resolution system, which staff turn to before placing their cases before the Tribunal. The period of 30 years having passed now makes this an appropriate time to conduct a full systemic review, which will provide an opportunity for benchmarking against contemporary best practice, as well as identifying areas for improvement for the benefit of both staff and the organization as a whole.

As international civil servants governed under ADB's administrative orders, staff do not have recourse to any national court or tribunal with respect to their disputes with their employer, ADB. ADB staff, therefore, expect that the dispute resolution system as a whole will meet all of the requirements that they would expect from any domestic employment dispute resolution in ADB member countries from which they all come. ADB staff have a right, therefore, to have all formal parts of the system, not just the final appeal at the level of the Tribunal, be truly independent, impartial, fair, and just. Compliance with natural justice and procedural fairness are expected. The remedies available should also mirror those available within ADB member countries. These include not only compensation, but also the option for restoration to a position where there was an improper termination.

It is to be noted that the United Nations (UN) had a similar system to that used by ADB, although there were minor differences. In 2006, the UN engaged a panel of experts to review its entire internal justice system. The review concluded that, below the level of the Appeals Tribunal—the highest level of formal appeal similar to ADB's Administrative Tribunal, there were serious issues in regard to independence and the expression of rights for staff members. The conclusion of the expert review panel was that the UN internal justice system was outmoded, dysfunctional, and ineffective, and that it lacked independence. The panel went on to find that:

> "Effective reform of the United Nations cannot happen without an efficient, independent and well-resourced internal justice system that will safeguard the rights of staff members and ensure the effective accountability of managers and staff members."[11]

There have been a number of systemic improvements to the informal aspects of the ADB internal justice system over the years. These include the establishment of the Office of Professional Conduct, the Ombuds Office, and compulsory conciliation. These place some of the matters which concerned the UN Redesign Panel outside of our area of concern. There are, however, serious issues of independence, accountability, and protection needing to be addressed within the

---

[11]   Redesign Panel on the United Nations System of Administration of Justice. 2006. *Report of the Redesign Panel of the United Nations System of Administration of Justice A/61/205.* https://digitallibrary.un.org/record/581262.

internal justice system. These include the following areas which reflect issues that have consistently been brought to the attention of the Staff Council:

- The leveling of the playing field of representation through the provision of legal representation for all staff members from the conciliation process through to final appeal. The bank at all times has highly trained and skilled lawyers acting for it and involved in every aspect of the review process.

- The introduction of a formal management review process with respect to challenged decisions. This would be the first part of the formal review process. Those undertaking the review cannot have anything whatsoever to do with the making of the challenged decision. The review process would look at issues of conformity with the required processes and reasonableness of the decision. This may result in very early dispute resolution.

- The replacement of the Appeals Committee with a totally independent body. The current system does not have the requisite level of fairness and independence. It cannot be viewed as impartial, and it is part of an outmoded system. It is suggested that a first instance formal review process be conducted by an independent international judge, sitting alone. Appeals of decisions from this level would be to the Tribunal. The judge should be an expert in administrative and employment law for international organizations, with at least 10 years of judicial experience, and should be appointed upon the recommendation of an independent expert committee.

- The default position regarding the consideration of a review at the judicial level should be a right to an actual hearing in person, which right should only be surrendered by agreement of the parties.

- Staff members challenging decisions should be provided with copies of all relevant documents leading to the decision being made. This will inform not only the staff members, but also the Tribunal of whether there has been full compliance with the legal requirements for each decision.

- An examination of the modality of appointment of judges to the Tribunal, with there being no direct involvement of either management or staff. Judges should ideally have at least 10 years international experience in administrative law for international organizations. When the Tribunal was established, there were few judges working internationally in the field as specialists in the area. This is no longer the case. Again, the judges should be appointed upon the recommendation of an independent expert committee.

- Accountability by reference to the ADB President for decision makers and staff members, where a decision has involved misfeasance of some kind.

- For the system to be fully approachable and functional, the issue of retaliation needs to be better addressed, with protection being provided for staff appealing certain decisions, whistleblowers, and those complaining of harassment and bullying. Such protection needs to be meaningfully applied in all resident missions, field offices, as well as at headquarters.

- Once a decision is made by the Tribunal, there should be no interference by management with such decision. Decisions should be implemented, unless the Tribunal is convinced that there are cogent reasons why it cannot be fully or practicably implemented, in which case damages would be payable to further compensate a staff member. Article X.1 of the Statute of the Administrative Tribunal should be amended to this effect. Where a decision has been found to have been made incorrectly, a staff member should not have their career ruined by management effectively supporting the erroneous decision.

On behalf of the ADB Staff Council and Staff Association, I offer my most sincere congratulations to the ADB Administrative Tribunal on celebrating this 30-year milestone, and hope that it too would express a view in support of an external review of the internal justice system. This would further strengthen belief in the system and build upon the rich experiences of the past 3 decades, growing from strength to strength as it supports ADB into the next 30 years. There is a great opportunity here for the ADB Administrative Tribunal to move forward on a foundation of trust, fairness, and accountability in fulfilling its important role, while also upholding the cultural values and rights of the organization to protect and safeguard the welfare and well-being of ADB's most valuable assets—its staff.

The ADB Administrative Tribunal— 30 Years of Operations

Christine Griffiths, Senior Attorney to the Administrative Tribunal

I. History of Establishment and Mandate

The Asian Development Bank (ADB or the bank), being a multilateral organization established by treaty in 1966 and having its headquarters in Manila, Philippines, is immune from the jurisdiction of the courts and government agencies of its member states. As a corollary to this immunity, ADB recognized that it needed to create an adequate dispute resolution system for the mutual benefit of staff members and the organization.

Prior to 1991, ADB had an internal appeal process against administrative decisions, but this was later considered inadequate. As a result, the Board of Directors of the bank decided to establish an appeal mechanism to which aggrieved staff members might have recourse after exhausting all internal means of redress of their grievance. The Board initially considered a single External Arbiter, but after a review of the framework, it was concluded that an Administrative Tribunal would be able to undertake a "more thorough and balanced examination of a case and would, through a certain distribution of nationalities, be perceived to render a more impartial judgement than a single arbiter."[12]

In April 1991, the ADB Administrative Tribunal (the Tribunal) was established. Its creation, through the Board of Directors' adoption of its Statute,[13] strengthened the rule of law in the bank's internal operations by providing a mechanism to review the actions of management to ensure that treatment of staff members was in compliance with the rules and regulations of the bank. It also enhanced the morale of staff and made the bank a more desirable and efficient place to work. The Tribunal was purposefully created in the image of the World Bank Administrative Tribunal (WBAT), the latter having been established 10 years earlier in 1981 (at the same time as the Inter-American Development Bank Administrative Tribunal). Other notable administrative tribunals already in existence at the time were the International Labour Organization Administrative Tribunal (ILOAT), established in 1946, and the United Nations Administrative Tribunal, established in 1949.

---

[12] ADB Board of Directors Paper. 11 April 1991.
[13] Statutes of the Administrative Tribunal of the Asian Development Bank (ADB Administrative Tribunal Statute).

With the creation of the Tribunal, decisions by management were to be subject to judicial review by a panel of external judges. The Tribunal hears and passes judgment upon any application in which an individual staff of the bank alleges nonobservance of the contract of employment or terms of appointment, which include all pertinent regulations and rules in force at the time of alleged nonobservance, as well as the provisions of the Staff Retirement Plan and the benefit plans provided by the bank to the staff.[14] In terms of composition, scope of judgments, and rules of procedure, the structure of the Tribunal system proposed and endorsed was in line with the practice of comparable organizations, such as the World Bank and the Inter-American Development Bank.

II.   Function and Procedure

The Tribunal began functioning in the beginning of 1992 according to its 1991 Statute. The Statute has since been amended twice. The first amendment was effective January 1995 and increased the number of judges at the Tribunal from three to five (the additional members not actually being elected until July 1995). This change made it possible to convene panels of three or five members, the latter being a "full panel." It also became possible for a judge to issue as an attachment an opinion dissenting from the Tribunal's decision (see section on *Dissenting Opinions* below). The second amendment was made effective 30 January 2006, creating the Committee on Administrative Tribunal Matters to advise on candidates for appointment to the Tribunal, and introducing the potential of the Applicant having to pay the bank's costs for defending a case if the Tribunal finds the application was "without foundation either in fact or under existing law" or "intended to delay the resolution of the case or to harass the Bank or any of its officers or employees."[15]

The Tribunal has conducted 47 sessions since its creation. It usually meets at least once a year, and sometimes twice a year, in order to decide disputes without any undue delay. It usually holds sessions in Manila at the bank's facilities, but it is not precluded, when necessary, from arranging a session in other locations. The Tribunal has done so in Colombo, New York, and Yokohama; it also conducted an evidentiary hearing in Tokyo. It has also held two sessions remotely, due to travel constraints caused by the COVID-19 pandemic.

The actual conduct of the proceedings is regulated mainly by the Tribunal's Rules of Procedure, established and adopted by the Tribunal in 1992 (and amended several times since).[16] Administrative Order No. 2.07 was issued to further explain the role and procedures of the Tribunal. The procedure during the written phase generally follows the normal legal procedure of international tribunals: the Application is filed with the Tribunal office and is sent to the bank which then,

---

[14]   Articles I and II of the Tribunal's Statute.
[15]   ADB Administrative Tribunal Statute, Article X, para. 6.
[16]   The Rules of Procedure were amended in September 1994, August 1995, and March 2021, and five new Practice Directions have been added since 2000.

as the Respondent, provides its written Answer to the Application within a time limit, which then leads to the opening of the second round of written comments consisting of the Applicant's Reply and the Respondent's Rejoinder. This round is optional for the parties to the case, but the Tribunal does have the power to make it obligatory for both parties, should it decide that such extra pleadings are necessary for the decision of the case. In any case, the second round of proceedings has been used in every case to date submitted to the Tribunal. If both parties and the Tribunal consider that the case is sufficiently pleaded and sufficient evidence of the issues has been gathered, then the Tribunal's rules allow that the case be decided without oral proceedings. The two rounds of pleadings for each party, supplemented by the typically dozens of annexed documents, usually provide an adequate basis for decision-making.

In most cases, the disputed issues—factual as well as legal—have been resolved without seeing live witnesses, and on the pleadings alone. There have been 11 occasions when requests for oral hearings were denied. While during the Tribunal's second decade, oral hearings were more common—four having been held between 2006 and 2009—there have been none held in the last decade. When the Tribunal has held hearings, which are in the Tribunal's discretion to grant, they have been considered useful in addressing very significant issues—by helping the Tribunal to elicit more evidence from witnesses and to hear arguments of counsel at greater length, and for the parties to have their "day in court." This was particularly the case at the first oral hearing conducted by the Tribunal to hear witnesses being examined and cross examined when alleged sexual harassment was at issue.[17]

Dissenting Opinions

Article IX of the Tribunal's Statute expressly grants to judges the right to issue a separate opinion, to be attached to the decision itself. There have been two lengthy dissenting opinions filed at the Tribunal. In one case, the Tribunal (4 to 1) upheld the bank's decision to make 60 the mandatory retirement age, but the dissenting judge strongly believed that this was a violation of staff rules and ADB practices, indicating that staff members were entitled to work until the age of 65.[18] In the second case, the Tribunal (3 to 2) sustained the bank's announcement of a policy not to pay tax reimbursement benefits to staff from the United States and the Philippines, in the face of an earlier Tribunal judgment that some construed as making such payments mandatory and unalterable. The dissenting judges contended that the Board of Directors should not decide to expressly prohibit tax reimbursement payments unless it likewise disavowed or expressly abandoned the principle of equal pay for equal work internally and externally.[19]

---

[17]   *Ms. X v. Asian Development Bank, Decision No. 74.* [2006]. 7 ADBAT p. 91.

[18]   *Samuel v. Asian Development Bank (No. 2), Decision No. 15.* [1996]. 2 ADBAT Reports p. 51; Stern dissenting at 69.

[19]   *Mesch and Siy v. Asian Development Bank (No. 4), Decision No. 35.* [1997]. 3 ADBAT Reports p. 71; Stern and Sawada dissenting at 93.

III.   Sources of Law

Traditionally, within the internal legal systems of intergovernmental organizations, the hierarchy of legal norms governs the legal relations between the staff member and the organization and arranges the administrative and judicial appeals system.[20] At the bank, the hierarchy of legal norms has at its highest level the Agreement Establishing the ADB, supplemented by the Agreement between the ADB and the Government of the Philippines regarding the Headquarters of the ADB, both agreements being treaties under international law. These are further regulated by lower-level norms; at ADB these are contained in the Staff Rules and Regulations issued by the Board of Directors, which are further specified and developed by lower-level administrative norms—administrative orders and circulars issued by management. However, some terms of employment may be specifically agreed upon in the employment contract. Furthermore, all administrative tribunals cite the rules developed in their own practice through earlier decisions, which has been the case with the Tribunal. Principles of "natural justice," such as due process of law, are often considered as well.

There is no general code of international civil service law, but the common law of the international civil service has come into existence, and the analogies which can be drawn from the decisions of other administrative tribunals have a great deal of guidance value. For example, the Tribunal has cited, in a few cases, the practice of the WBAT and the ILOAT as having guidance value.

On rare occasions, there may be a conflict between the express directives of the bank, clearly stated to be a part of the staff member's "contract of employment," and more general commonly accepted principles of law. When that conflict cannot readily be resolved, the latter principles will commonly prevail. An example is a case decided by the Tribunal in 1997, known as the *Amora* case.[21] Mr. Amora, a Filipino, worked over the course of 15 consecutive years as a member of the supporting staff in ADB's printing office. His initial appointment was for 1 year, and it described Mr. Amora as an "independent contractor" and as such "not be entitled to any compensation, allowances, benefits or rights from or against the Bank other than expressly provided therein." He was not included in ADB's pension plan. The bank kept Mr. Amora on a series of 1-year and other very short-term renewals and extensions for 15 years and he was 'regularized' only 2 years before his mandatory retirement age. This meant he was forced to retire with a very small pension. Mr. Amora's request to be accorded pension rights for the full 15 years of his service as a so-called "independent contractor" was denied by the bank, and his case ultimately reached the Tribunal. The Tribunal concluded that the legal relationship the bank sought to create simply by using the term "independent contractor" fundamentally disregarded reality. Mr. Amora was an employee of ADB with regular, essentially unchanging full-time job responsibilities, working subject to the directives of ADB supervisors. The

---

[20]   In *re de Merode Decision No. 1.* [1981], the WBAT reports "it must apply the internal law of the Bank as the law governing the conditions of employment."

[21]   *Amora v. Asian Development Bank, Decision No. 24.* [1997]. 3 ADBAT p. 1.

Tribunal held that the use of short-term contracts which denied him benefits was a *detournement de pouvoir* or abuse of power, and set aside the 1-year contracts as not reflecting the true relationship between the bank and the staff member.

IV.   The Appeals System: How the Steps Below and the Tribunal Operate

Similar to many other international organizations, the appeals system of the bank has two phases: (i) administrative and (ii) judicial.

One condition for the jurisdiction of the Tribunal to be triggered, except by agreement or by the Tribunal's discretion in exceptional cases, is that the Applicant must have first completed compulsory conciliation and then sought administrative review from which a decision must be issued. The bank has also established the Appeals Committee to hear and deal with the allegations regarding administrative decisions which, allegedly, have been influenced by administrative irregularities or abnormalities. The Appeals Committee is composed of fellow staff members, not necessarily lawyers, some nominated by management and some nominated by the Staff Council. They conduct a full evidentiary and adversary proceeding and make recommendations to the ADB President as to how to resolve the dispute. The proceedings before the Appeals Committee are not binding on either the staff member or the bank. If the staff member remains dissatisfied after action upon an Appeals Committee recommendation, he or she may file an application with the Tribunal. But the nonuse of the procedures at the Appeal Committee creates, under ordinary circumstances, a situation of non-exhaustion of internal remedies, which according to Article II, para. 3 (a) of the Tribunal's Statute would preclude the application from the Tribunal's jurisdiction.[22]

These "steps below" are designed to encourage disputes to be resolved before they come to the Tribunal. To this end, the structural design appears to be working, as one can see from examining the number of disputes at the start of the process (compulsory conciliation) to the smaller number that remain contested after the appeals process and thereafter proceeding to the Tribunal. For example, in 2006, of 12 cases that went to conciliation, 6 proceeded to the Tribunal. Similarly in 2007, of 11 cases at the conciliation stage, only 5 went to the Tribunal; in 2008, of 3 cases disputed at the administrative stage, only 2 proceeded to the Tribunal; and in 2009, of 3 cases that commenced at the conciliation stage, none proceeded to the Tribunal. Between 2015 and 2018, of 10 cases that went to conciliation, only 5 proceeded to the Tribunal; and between 2018 and 2020, of 8 cases that went to conciliation, only 1 proceeded to the Tribunal.

The judicial phase of the appeals system in ADB consists only of one-level legal proceedings. The Statute of the Tribunal establishes the Tribunal as the final

---

[22]   Article II of the Tribunal's Statute; See also *Zimonyi v. Asian Development Bank, Decision No. 13.* [1996]. 2 ADBAT Reports p. 43; *Jianming Xu v. Asian Development Bank, Decision No. 25.* [2005]. 7 ADBAT Reports p. 27.

independent appeal mechanism for the resolution of employment disputes between the bank's management and its staff members.[23] As is usual for most other international organizations, there is no higher legal (appellate) level to which an ADBAT decision may be appealed.[24] The Tribunal's judgments are final and binding,[25] and only limited revision and reopening of the case before the Tribunal itself are allowed.

V.   Composition

Since 1 January 1995, the Tribunal has been composed of five members who are required to be nationals of ADB member countries, but no two of whom may be nationals of the same member country. Each must possess the qualifications required for appointment to high judicial office or be jurisconsults of recognized competence.[26]

The members of the Tribunal are appointed by ADB's Board of Directors from a list of candidates, or in the case of a single vacancy, the one candidate, recommended by the President after consideration by the bank's Committee on Administrative Tribunal Matters (an organ that includes at least the General Counsel, the Secretary, and the Chair of the Staff Council).[27] A member is appointed for a term of 3 years, which, if not otherwise specifically decided by the Board of Directors, begins on the first day of October of the year of appointment. The number of terms for each member's appointment is limited to three terms.[28] Reappointment is upon the President's recommendation, and in practice, three terms has been the norm to ensure a high degree of continuity.

So far 24 persons have served as members of the Tribunal. Their expertise reflects both knowledge from the practical legal field, either at the international level or at the national level, and expertise from the academic world. The majority of the members (at least 13) have had, or still have, high academic posts, and several members also possess experience from other administrative tribunals (8), mainly having been members of the WBAT or the ILOAT. Seven members have been members of Supreme Courts in their own countries or international courts. Fourteen judges have been from regional member countries, and 10 have been from non-regional countries, those being the Philippines (3), Japan (4), India (2), Pakistan (1), Sri Lanka (1), Singapore (1), Australia (1), New Zealand (1), the United States (4), France (1), the United Kingdom (2), Belgium (1), Finland (1), and the Netherlands (1).

---

[23]   ADB Administrative Tribunal Statute, Articles I and II.
[24]   The UN is an exception having the UN Appeals Tribunal as a second-level appellate review tribunal.
[25]   ADB Administrative Tribunal Statute, Article IX.
[26]   ADB Administrative Tribunal Statute, Article IV, para. 1.
[27]   ADB Administrative Tribunal Statute, Article IV, para. 2, as amended in 2006. The Staff Council is the only employees' organization.
[28]   ADB Administrative Tribunal Statute, Article IV, para. 3.

Seven of the 24 members of the Tribunal have been women; and 3 of them have served as President—Justice Flerida Romero and Professor Gillian Triggs each served one term as President, and Justice Lakshmi Swaminathan served two terms as President. For a while, the Tribunal was the only (and first) international administrative tribunal to have a majority of women in its composition (Judges Swaminathan, Trebilcock, and Triggs), and did so while also serving with a woman as President (Justice Swaminathan).

The first set of judges sat on the Tribunal from 1991 to 1995. Professor Elihu Lauterpacht, CBE, QC, then Director of the Research Centre of the University of Cambridge (later also President of the WBAT and judge ad hoc before the International Court of Justice) was elected President of the Tribunal. The other judges were Philippine Supreme Court Justice Florentino Feliciano (later Judge of the Appellate Body of the World Trade Organization in Geneva, Judge of the WBAT, and during a later term, President of the Tribunal), and Sri Lankan Supreme Court Justice Mark D. H. Fernando (later also judge at the ILOAT and President of the Tribunal). With the resignation of Judges Lauterpacht and Feliciano, four new members (membership having been increased from three to five in 1995) were appointed: (i) Professor Brigitte Stern of the University of Paris I (later Judge at the United Nations Administrative Tribunal); (ii) Dr. Laxmi Singhvi who was India's High Commissioner to London; (iii) Professor Toshio Sawada of Sophia University; and (iv) Professor Robert Gorman of the University of Pennsylvania Law School, one of the founding judges of the WBAT (and later President of the WBAT and the Tribunal).

Two new judges were appointed to the Tribunal in 1996, and another in 1997. Professor Stern was replaced by Professor Martti Koskenniemi of the University of Helsinki; Dr. Singhvi by Dr. Thio Su Mien, former law dean and private practitioner in Singapore and later judge of the WBAT; and Professor Sawada by Professor Shinya Murase, also from Sophia University.

In October 2001, Philippine Supreme Court Justice and ILOAT Judge Flerida Romero (later President of the Tribunal) replaced Dr. Thio Su Mien; and in August 2003, former Punjab High Court Judge Supreme Court Justice Khaja Samdani replaced Mark Fernando. In October 2003, Martti Koskenniemi was replaced by a private practitioner in Belgium, Claude Wantiez; and in August 2004, two judges, Professor Gorman and Professor Shinya Murase, were replaced by Arnold Zack, labor arbitrator of Harvard University and former President of the National Academy of Arbitrators (later President of the Tribunal), and Professor Yuji Iwasawa of the University of Tokyo and later Chairperson of the UN Human Rights Committee. In October 2006, Justice Romero was replaced by former Tribunal Judge and retired Justice of the Supreme Court of the Philippines, Justice Florentino Feliciano, who in turn ended his third and final term on 30 September 2009 and replaced in February 2010 by former Vice-Chairman (Judicial) of the Central Administrative Tribunal, India and former Joint-Secretary of the Indian Ministry of Law and Justice, Lakshmi Swaminathan (later President of the Tribunal).

In October 2012, two judges, Claude Wantiez and Judge Samdani, were replaced by Gillian Triggs, Professor of Melbourne University and President of the Australian Human Rights Commission (later President of the Tribunal), and Roy Lewis, a private practitioner in the United Kingdom. In October 2014, Professor Iwasawa was replaced by Samuel Estreicher, a private practitioner in the United States, for one session, before in turn being replaced by Professor Shin-ichi Ago of Ritsumeikan University (current President of the Tribunal). In January and October of 2015, Judges Zack and Lewis were replaced by international law practitioners Judge Anne Trebilcock of the United States and Judge Chris de Cooker of the Netherlands. In April of 2019, former ADBAT Executive Secretary and International Criminal Court Judge Raul Pangalangan replaced Judge Swaminathan. The most recent appointment to the Tribunal was Judge Silvia Cartwright, former High Court Judge and Governor General for New Zealand.

VI.   Types of Disputes

Over its 30-year history, the Tribunal has issued 125 decisions. Eighty-four percent (84%) of applications filed concerned staff members contesting administrative decisions that affect them. The remaining 16% were related to applications for the interpretation or revision of earlier decisions. These cases are published both on ADB's website and in the Tribunal's own reports, published by the Office of the Executive Secretary. There are now 10 volumes of the reports.

The appeals in these cases have focused on certain substantive issues, but at the same time, several important procedural questions have also been decided. The types of disputes brought to the Tribunal in order of frequency include the following:

- Conflict resulting from job classification and career development

    These decisions challenged by staff members concern disputed selection and promotion procedures, job classifications, transfers, promotions, and career development, and account for 27% of applications. The first decision rendered by the Tribunal involved the non-conversion of the Applicant's contract into a regular appointment. The Tribunal found that the bank's decision was invalidated by its failure to apply due process. It also laid down the guiding principle by which it would review management decisions that are discretionary in nature, the applicable test being whether such a decision has been "arbitrary, discriminatory, or improperly motivated, or has been carried out in violation of a fair and reasonable procedure."[29] Another notable case examined the evolution of the performance evaluation system in relation to the Applicant contesting a new performance management system that required a certain distribution of ratings. In that case, the Tribunal decided it was

---

[29]   *Lindsey v. Asian Development Bank, Decision No. 1.* [1992]. 1 ADBAT Reports p. 1.

not persuaded that there were "fixed" quotas, or that if there were such, that they were applied to the Applicant.[30]

- Disputes related to performance evaluation

The challenges of these decisions range from termination of appointment, non-confirmation of appointment at the end of the probationary period, to irregularities in performance evaluation by supervisors. Of these, five involved harassment and discrimination issues.[31] They represent 22% of applications. The Tribunal resolved its first performance evaluation case at its second session in 1994 and found that the staff member's performance evaluation report scores did not reflect his true rating, due to an informal quota of "distinguished" ratings.[32]

- Violation of ADB rules and regulations, and conditions of employment

These cases account for 22% of applications and concern disputes relating to the mandatory retirement age (which elicited several claims), equal pay for equal work, the duty of reasonable care, the Staff Retirement Plan, changes to the Group Medical Insurance Plan to ensure its long-term viability,[33] and changes to education assistance benefits provided to international staff.[34] Three of the more significant cases brought to the Tribunal, the *Mesch and Siy*, *Samuel*, and *Perrin* cases, are discussed in detail below. Two other cases required the Tribunal to examine the responsibility of an international organization for the safety of its officials and decide whether the bank had met its duty to exercise reasonable care. The *Bares*[35] case arose from the murder of a lawyer of the bank in its basement parking area at the hands of a member of its security contingent. The Tribunal, finding that the claim was based on contract and not on vicarious liability arising from tort, held that any supposed defects in the bank's security system could not have prevented the tragic event, and that the bank had met its duty to exercise reasonable care in its selection and supervision of the security company employed. The second case, *Chang et al.*,[36] contested the bank's selection and supervision of its in-house medical facility operated by Associated Medical and Clinical Services Inc. (AMCSI) when the initial Applicant was diagnosed late with lung cancer and later died. In that case, the Tribunal was also not persuaded that there had been a breach of duty of care in the selection and supervision of AMCSI.

[30] *Zeki Kiy v. Asian Development Bank, Decision No. 89.* [2009]. 8 ADBAT Reports p. 189.
[31] *Alexander v. Asian Development Bank, Decision No. 40.* [1998]. 4 ADBAT Reports p. 41; *Yamagishi v. Asian Development Bank, Decision No. 65.* [2004]. 6 ADBAT Reports p. 107; *Ms. X v. Asian Development Bank, Decision No. 74.* [2006]. 7 ADBAT Reports p. 91; *Ms. A v. Asian Development Bank, Decision No. 87.* [2009]. 8 ADBAT Reports p. 155; and *Mr. Y v. Asian Development Bank, Decision No. 94.* [2011].
[32] *Tay Sin Yan v. Asian Development Bank, Decision No. 3.* [1994]. 1 ADBAT Reports p. 35.
[33] *Suzuki et al. v. Asian Development Bank, Decision No. 82.* [2007]. 8 ADBAT Reports p. 59.
[34] *Perrin et al. No. 3 v. Asian Development Bank, Decision No. 113.* [2018]. 10 ADBAT Reports p. 194.
[35] *Bares et al. v. Asian Development Bank, Decision No. 5.* [1995]. 1 ADBAT Reports p. 53.
[36] *Chang et al. v. Asian Development Bank, Decision No. 84.* [2008]. 8 ADBAT Reports p. 87.

- Disputes related to disciplinary action

  These cases represent 16% of applications, the majority of which involved dismissal of the Applicant. The misconduct involved ranged from fraudulent telephone calls[37] and medical insurance claims,[38] bid manipulation,[39] theft,[40] forgery of documents,[41] misappropriation of property,[42] rental subsidy fraud,[43] writing and sending e-mails that damaged ADB's reputation,[44] filing a criminal complaint with the local Philippine courts,[45] to availing of tax-exempt privileges through fraudulent misrepresentation.[46]

- Disputes related to payment of entitlements

  These disputes were related to payment of entitlements such as rental subsidy, the special separation program, and expatriate benefits. They represent 13% of applications. Five cases involved each Applicant contesting the denial of their early retirement under the bank's voluntary early retirement program known as the Special Separation Program. The Tribunal concluded that the Applicants were ineligible, but awarded compensation in each case as they agreed that the formulating criteria and their implementation were flawed and that this had meant their wrongful deprivation of a qualifying opportunity.[47] Another case involved 29 professional Filipino staff alleging discrimination with respect to certain employment benefits and remuneration extended to expatriate staff but not to themselves. The Applicants alleged they were similarly situated, so the decision involved the Tribunal interpreting the principle of equal treatment. Their claim was upheld with regard to two benefits, *force majeure* protection and education grants, but rejected with regard to two other benefits, home leave and separation pay.[48]

In its most recent decade of operation, the Tribunal has seen a slight increase in the number of disputes relating to conditions of employment (from 18% in its first 20 years of operation to 22% over its 30-year history). In the 125 cases decided so far, relief was either fully or partially granted in 37% of cases; and applications were dismissed or denied in 68 cases (this included 15 denials of

[37]   *Zaidi v. Asian Development Bank, Decision No. 17.* [1996]. 2 ADBAT Reports p. 89; *Chaudhry v. Asian Development Bank, Decision No. 23.* [1996]. 2 ADBAT Reports p. 171.

[38]   *Abat v. Asian Development Bank, Decision No. 78.* [2007]. 8 ADBAT Reports p. 1.

[39]   *Domdom Jr. v. Asian Development Bank, Decision No. 47.* [2000]. 5 ADBAT Reports p. 37.

[40]   *Galang v. Asian Development Bank, Decision No. 55.* [2002]. 6 ADBAT Reports p. 25.

[41]   *Ms. C v. Asian Development Bank, Decision No. 58.* [2003]. 6 ADBAT Reports p. 71.

[42]   *Lim v. Asian Development Bank, Decision No. 76.* [2006]. 7 ADBAT Reports p. 127.

[43]   *Bristol v. Asian Development Bank, Decision No. 75.* [2006]. 7 ADBAT Reports p. 113; *De Alwis 4 v. Asian Development Bank, Decision No. 85.* [2008]. 8 ADBAT Reports p. 108.

[44]   *Hua Du v. Asian Development Bank, Decision No. 101.* [2013]. IX ADBAT Reports p. 82.

[45]   *Mr. H v. Asian Development Bank, Decision No. 108.* [2017]. X ADBAT Reports p. 110.

[46]   *Ms. J v. Asian Development Bank, Decision No. 116.* [2018]. X ADBAT Reports p. 247; *Mr. K v. Asian Development Bank, Decision No. 117.* [2018]. X ADBAT Reports p. 274; *Ms. L v. Asian Development Bank, Decision No. 118.* [2018]. X ADBAT Reports p. 308; *Ms. M v. Asian Development Bank, Decision No. 119.* [2018]. X ADBAT Reports p. 345.

[47]   *Breckner v. Asian Development Bank, Decision No. 25.* [1997]. 3 ADBAT Reports p. 17.

[48]   *De Armas et al. v. Asian Development Bank, Decision No. 39.* [1998]. 4 ADBAT Reports p. 9.

revision of clarification). Of the 125 applications, 7 were considered inadmissible, and 4 cases were withdrawn due to an agreed upon settlement.

Significant decisions early in the Tribunal's history were the four *Mesch and Siy* cases, which involved discussion of essential and nonessential conditions of employment—with the essential conditions of employment being so "fundamental and essential" that the bank is forbidden from changing them to the detriment of staff members, whereas the nonessential conditions of employment can be unilaterally changed by management subject to certain limitations related to expectations. The *Mesch and Siy* cases were about the reimbursement of taxes paid by Mr. Mesch (American) and Mr. Siy (Filipino) on their bank income. Most governments, as a matter of informal comity, do not impose a tax upon their citizens' income from international organizations. However, the United States and the Philippines are among the very few nations that do collect income taxes from their nationals working at ADB. This results in a net income for a US or Filipino citizen that is less than another nation's citizen doing precisely the same type of work.

In its initial decision, the Tribunal held that the bank's own articulated principle of equal pay for comparable work was an unchangeable essential condition of employment. The Tribunal applied that principle and concluded, even in the absence of any previous program of tax reimbursement, and in the absence of any ADB statements confirming such a program in any way, that tax reimbursement was a condition of employment. The Tribunal therefore ordered appropriate compensation to the United States and Filipino staff for the 2 past years that were in dispute. But there was no precise holding that tax reimbursement was fundamental and unchangeable.[49] As a result, the ADB Board of Directors adopted a resolution to the effect that "the Bank shall not reimburse the taxes paid by any ..... staff member of the Bank for the taxes paid by them on their salaries and emoluments paid by the Bank, effective upon the date of this Resolution."

When Messrs. Mesch and Siy returned to the Tribunal, it was not surprising for them to argue that tax reimbursement, designed to achieve equal pay for equal work, was a fundamental and an essential term, that the bank was legally obligated not only to pay it for the past but to continue it in the future, and that the Board of Directors' resolution was therefore invalid. The three Tribunal judges who constituted the majority distinguished the *de Merode* WBAT decision and held,[50] particularly because of the absence of any past practice or confirming statements by ADB with respect to tax reimbursement, that such reimbursement was a non-fundamental and nonessential condition of employment subject to complete withdrawal by the ADB Board of Directors. The majority concluded that although there was indeed a fundamental principle of equal pay for equal work, the equality requirement could be satisfied by equal compensation before the imposition of national income taxes, which was a circumstance over which the bank had no control.[51]

---

49 *Mesch and Siy v. Asian Development Bank, Decision No. 2.* [1994]. 1 ADBAT Reports p. 21.
50 *de Merode, Decision No. 1.* [1981]. WBAT Reports.
51 *Mesch and Siy v. Asian Development Bank, No. 4, Decision No. 35.* [1997]. 3 ADBAT Reports p. 71.

Another significant decision of the Tribunal was on the *Samuel*[52] case, which challenged the Board of Governors' policy decision of reducing the prevailing mandatory retirement age of staff members from 65 to 60. The Applicant asserted that such a change was an abuse of discretion, while the bank argued that it was beyond the power of the Tribunal to review a decision of the Board of Directors, the bank's highest decision-making authority. The Tribunal rejected the latter position. It held that even the Board is subject to the rule of law and has limits upon the exercise of its discretion. Nonetheless, the Tribunal upheld the change in the mandatory retirement age; it was viewed as within the Board's discretion, as not unreasonable or arbitrary, and as consistent with prevailing bank procedures and other more general principles of procedural law. This case also saw the Tribunal's first dissenting opinion.

A more recent significant decision of the Tribunal was on the *Perrin et al. (No. 3)* case,[53] which challenged the changes to education assistance benefits provided to international staff as part of a broader revision of the bank's compensation and benefits package for all staff. These changes were implemented in the context of the ADB Strategy 2020 after a year-long consultation period. The Tribunal first identified which of the Applicants had *jurisdiction personae* by determining those who were directly and adversely affected on an individual basis by the changes. It then rejected the Applicants' assertion that the changes could not be unilaterally made by the bank, as it held that, while education assistance may be a fundamental and essential element of their employment contract, the same could not be said concerning the details thereof. It also held that the bank had not violated any acquired rights of the Applicants nor acted in breach of its obligations toward its staff. In saying so, the Tribunal, in line with *Suzuki*,[54] decided that (i) the objective of the change was rational and legitimate, (ii) there was evidence to support the different treatment of various member groups, (iii) there was a rational nexus between the classification of persons subject to the differential treatment and the objective of the classification, and (iv) the differential treatment was proportionate to the objective of the change.

VII.   Relief and Compensation

The Statute provides that the following remedies are available: rescission of the decision contested, specific performance of the obligation invoked, or, in lieu of specific performance and at the option of the bank (if the ADB President decides it is in the interest of the bank to compensate the Applicant without further action), payment of compensation.[55]

In its first judgment rendered, in December 1992, the Tribunal, citing precedent from the World Bank Tribunal, read its remedial powers to include a choice

---

[52]   *Samuel v. Asian Development Bank, No. 2, Decision No. 15*. [1996]. 2 ADBAT Reports p. 51.

[53]   *Perrin et al. v. Asian Development Bank, No. 3, Decision No. 113*. [2018]. 10 ADBAT Reports p. 194.

[54]   *Suzuki v. Asian Development Bank, Decision No. 82*. [2008]. VIII ADBAT Reports p. 59.

[55]   Article X para. 1 of the Tribunal's Statute.

among rescission of the contested decision, specific performance or, in its place, compensation—the power to grant compensation for injury caused.[56] But the subsequent decision[57] stressed that the Tribunal cannot affirmatively exercise a discretionary power belonging to the bank, and therefore substitute the Tribunal's judgment for that of the bank (e.g., a direction to grant a performance rating, merit pay increase, or promotion). Instead, the Tribunal is limited to setting aside the defective decision and, where applicable, remanding the issue to the bank for proper consideration. A recent decision was made for the *Ibrahim* case, which saw the Tribunal exercise its power to rescind the Applicant's "unsatisfactory" rating and order either the Applicant's reinstatement to her former position being made whole for all losses, or her payment of compensation without further action being taken.[58]

Cases where specific performance has been an option include the *Mesch and Siy*[59] case wherein the Tribunal ordered the bank to reimburse the Applicants the amount of the income tax levied against and paid on their salaries beginning from the year 1990, together with interest of 5% per annum, beginning from 10 February 1992, for the years 1990 and 1991. The interpretation of the decision, together with certain related issues, was also later submitted for the Tribunal's consideration in *Ferdinand P. Mesch and Siy No. 2* case, in which the Tribunal ordered the bank to pay the Applicant immediately, plus interest on any remaining balance of their tax reimbursement still outstanding concerning those years at issue.

Despite having the actual claim dismissed, in several instances, the Tribunal has ordered compensation where it has found a violation of due process, for example, in the case of breach of confidentiality in the disciplinary cases of *Zaidi* and *Chaudhry*.[60] In one exceptional case, the *Bares* case, even where the bank was not found liable, the Tribunal recommended in a "rider" to its decision that due to the exceptional circumstances of the case, an *ex-gratia* payment be provided by the bank to the members of the deceased's family.

VIII. Conclusion

As of 30 June 2021, ADB had 2,332 staff, of whom 1,327 were international staff from 55 countries out of the 68 ADB members. The remainder were primarily Filipino support staff. Given this large number of staff from different cultures, it is not surprising that disputes would arise between them and their superiors or other representatives of management. The Tribunal has played and will continue to play an important role in supporting the rule of law in ADB's internal operations and providing a mechanism to solve internal disputes such that the

---

[56]   *Lindsey v. Asian Development Bank, Decision No. 1.* [1992]. 1 ADBAT Reports p. 1.

[57]   *Tay Sin Yan v. Asian Development Bank, Decision No. 3.* [1994]. 1 ADBAT Reports p. 35.

[58]   *Ibrahim v. Asian Development Bank, Decision No. 86.* [2008]. 8 ADBAT Reports p. 115.

[59]   *Mesch and Siy v. Asian Development Bank, Decision No. 2.* [1994]. 1 ADBAT Reports p. 21.

[60]   *Zaidi v. Asian Development Bank, Decision No. 17.* [1996]. 2 ADBAT Reports p. 89; *Chaudhry v. Asian Development Bank, Decision No. 23.* [1996]. 2 ADBAT Reports p. 171.

observation of staff's basic legal rights and the proper administration of justice can be guaranteed. It has also had an impact on the internal functioning of ADB— one notable example is the Tribunal acting as a catalyst for reviewing the bank's performance management system.

The Tribunal strives to act as an impartial arbiter whose decisions will hopefully be generally accepted by the bank and its staff as fair and just. Its decisions also appear to have provided a positive addition to the repertoire of jurisprudence of international administrative law in line with those of the World Bank, International Labour Organization, United Nations, International Monetary Fund, Inter-American Development Bank, and other intergovernmental agencies. The Tribunal is proud of its work and gratified to be able to celebrate its 30 years of operation.

ADB Administrative Tribunal and Remedies—Reliefs

Judge Lakshmi Swaminathan
Former President, ADB Administrative Tribunal

Introduction

International administrative tribunals have been constituted by many international organizations. They are judicial bodies that are quite distinct from a particular international organization. These administrative tribunals perform only judicial functions, in accordance with the statutes constituting the tribunals. Not very long ago, between 1940 and 1980, there were in operation two major international administrative tribunals, namely the United Nations Administrative Tribunal (UNAT) and the International Labour Organization Administrative Tribunal (ILOAT). The UNAT has become a two-tier judicial system. However, from 1980 onward, over 15 international administrative tribunals have been established by many international organizations and are operating today. Administrative tribunals have been set up by a number of international organizations, including international financial institutions and international banks, like the World Bank Administrative Tribunal (WBAT), which was established by the Board of Governors by statute in 1980, and the International Monetary Fund Administrative Tribunal (IMFAT) established by the IMF Board of Governors by statute in 1992.

An administrative tribunal is generally established by statute by the competent authority of a particular organization. It is an independent judicial forum of last resort for settlement of disputes submitted by the staff of the organization, who allege nonobservance of their contract of employment or of terms and conditions of appointment by the organization, in accordance with the provisions of the statute. The tribunal's decisions are final and binding. Normally the administrative tribunal exercises only the powers conferred by the statute. The question arises whether administrative tribunals have equitable jurisdiction or only that which has been conferred by statute, and as to how the compensation is to be computed.

The ADB Administrative Tribunal (ADBAT or the Tribunal) was established by the ADB Board of Directors under the Statute of the bank, effective from 1 April 1991. The Rules of the Tribunal were published effective from 1 January 1992. The Statute and the Rules of the Tribunal have been amended from time to time by the ADB Board of Directors. The Tribunal hears and passes judgment upon any application by which an individual "member of the staff" of the bank alleges nonobservance of the contract of employment or terms of appointment of such staff member. A "member of the staff" has been defined in Article 11(2) of the

Statute to include any current or former member of the bank staff who holds or has held a regular appointment or a fixed-term appointment of 2 years or more.

The Tribunal is an independent judicial forum and is composed of five members, including the President, who are nationals of ADB member countries. The members of the Tribunal exercise their duties totally independent of the bank, in the resolution of employment disputes arising between the bank and its staff members, in accordance with the provisions of the Statute of 1991, read with the Rules of Procedure and Practice Directions, 1992, as amended from time to time.

Any litigant/Applicant in a case, either before a Court or a Tribunal, seeks the remedies he/she prays for, but what he/she finally succeeds at getting is what is material and important. The Applicant who seeks any remedy before the Tribunal has to file an application to the Tribunal, in accordance with the provisions of the Tribunal's Statute and Rule 6 of the Rules of Procedure.

I.   Types of Remedies Provided under the ADBAT Statute, 1991

If the ADBAT comes to the conclusion that an application is well-founded, it can order the reliefs set out in Article X of the Statute, which reads:

> "1.   ..... it shall order the rescission of the decision contested or the specific performance of the obligation invoked. At the same time the Tribunal shall fix the amount of compensation to be paid to the Applicant for the injury sustained should the President of the Bank, within thirty days of the notification of the judgement, decide, in the interest of the Bank, that the Applicant shall be compensated without further action being taken in the case; provided that such compensation may not exceed the equivalent of three years' basic salary of the Applicant. The Tribunal may, however, in exceptional circumstances, when it considers it justified, order the payment of a higher compensation. A statement of the specific reasons for such an order shall be made.
>
> 2.   If the Tribunal concludes that an application is well-founded in whole or in part, it may order that the reasonable costs incurred by the Applicant in the case, including the cost of Applicant's counsel, be totally or partially borne by the bank, taking into account the nature and complexity of the case, the nature and quality of the work performed, and the amount of the fees in relation to prevailing rates.
>
> 3.   Should the Tribunal find that a procedure prescribed in the rules of the bank has not been observed, it may, at the request of the President of the bank and prior to the determination of the merits, order the case to be remanded for institution or correction of the required procedure.

4.   In all applicable cases, compensation and reasonable costs fixed by the Tribunal pursuant to paras. 1 and 2 of this Article shall be paid by the bank.

5.   The filing of an application shall not have the effect of suspending execution of the decision contested."

(Para. 6 of Article X has been dealt with below in para. 63).

II.   Applicant to Exhaust All "Other Remedies"

An Applicant wanting to seek any remedy before the Tribunal must first exhaust all other remedies available within the bank, as provided in Article 11, para. 3 of the Statute. It is only after the President of the bank has given a final decision regarding the complaint, that the application may be filed in the Tribunal. However, if the Applicant and the President of the bank agree to submit the application directly to the Tribunal, they may do so in exceptional circumstances, subject to the decision of the Tribunal.

III.   Applicant to Seek All Reliefs

Further, under Rule 6(3) of the Rules of Procedure, the Applicant instituting proceedings in the Tribunal has to indicate all the measures and decisions which the Applicant is requesting the Tribunal to order or take. This will include any preliminary or provisional measures, like production of documents; the decisions which the Applicant is contesting and seeking rescission under Article X, para. 1 of the Statute; the obligations which the Applicant is invoking and the specific performance; the amount of compensation the Applicant seeks in accordance with the option given to the President of the bank under Article X para. 1 of the Statute, and any other relief which the Applicant may request in accordance with the Statute.[61]

The Statute of the Tribunal states the remedial powers that can be granted by the Tribunal, in rather general terms, and the Tribunal has to quantify the amount of compensation which is just and fair. The expression "compensation" is widely used; sometimes the Tribunal refers to it as "reasonable compensation." The principle of "compensation" will require the Tribunal to adjudicate an amount by way of damages to be paid to the Applicant, so as to place the Applicant in a position as if they had not suffered that particular injury in the first instance, for example, by way of restoration or restitution. Normally, the compensation may not exceed the equivalent of 3-year basic salary of the Applicant, but for reasons to be recorded, higher compensation may be ordered by the Tribunal if it considers it justified. So far, the Tribunal has not granted compensation exceeding 3 years of

---

[61]   This is already Rule 6(4) of the Rules of Procedure effective 10 February 2021.

basic pay to the Applicant. In interpreting the statutory provisions, the Tribunal applies the general principles of common law and equity.

IV.   Some Frequently Requested Preliminary Pleas

The Applicant has to indicate any preliminary measures he/she is requesting the Tribunal to order before proceeding to consider the merits. Examples are (i) additional documents; (ii) oral hearing; (iii) confidentiality; (iv) "exceptional circumstances," where the Applicant and the bank agree to submit the application directly to the Tribunal, under Article 11(3); and (v) Hearing by the Tribunal *en banc*. Some decisions of the Tribunal on these requests are referred to below.

In *Mr. F v. ADB, ADBAT Reports, Vol. X*, [Decision No. 104, Decided on 6 August 2014] the Applicant's request for documentation was met which was supplied by the Respondent in the Annexes to the Answer. The request for confidentiality in respect of the Applicant's name was uncontested by the Respondent and granted by the Tribunal. Further, the Applicant had requested that a full panel be constituted to hear his Application.

The Tribunal was of the opinion that "there are no circumstances of sufficient novelty, complexity or difficulty to make it necessary or desirable that this case be considered by a panel consisting of all its Members." In the circumstances of the case, having regard to Article 5, para. 5 of the Statute, the Tribunal rejected the Applicant, *Mr. F*'s request for a full panel in Decision No. 104.

In another case, *Ms. G (No. 2) v. ADB, ADBAT Reports, Vol. X*, [Decision No. 107, Decided on 19 August 2016], the Tribunal found that the Application warranted a hearing *en banc* under the aforesaid provisions of the Statute.

In the case of *Maria Lourdes Drilon v. ADB, ADBAT Reports, Vol. X*, [Decision No. 110, Decided on 6 May 2017], under Practice Direction No. 3 of the Tribunal's Rules of Procedure, the Respondent had requested confidentiality of the name of the Applicant's supervisor. The Tribunal granted this in view of the sensitivity of the issues and the fact that he was still an officer in the Bank.

With regard to the request by an Applicant for an oral hearing (see for example, *Claus v. ADB, ADBAT Reports, Vol. X*, [Decision No. 105, Decided on 13 February, 2015], the Tribunal reiterated the position that under Article VIII of the Statute, "it is for the Tribunal to take a decision in each case whether oral proceedings are warranted or not; and this has to be read with the provisions of Rule 14 of the Rules of Procedure, which provide that 'Oral proceedings, including the presentation and examination of witness or experts may be held only if the Tribunal so decides.'" Taking into account the nature of the allegations made by the Applicant and the very extensive and detailed comments with supporting documents given by her and the Bank to substantiate their arguments, the Tribunal after due deliberation decided that oral proceedings were not warranted in this case.

In *Claus v. ADB*, (*supra* para. 22) the Applicant and Respondent made a joint application on 10 April 2014 to the Tribunal that pleaded there were "exceptional circumstances" under paragraph 3 of Article 11 of the Statute, despite internal remedies not having been exhausted for all five decisions that were challenged. By Order dated 14 April 2014, the joint request of the parties was allowed by the Tribunal i.e., to submit the Application to it. This relief is an "exception" as the Statute itself states.

In the Application dated 7 February 2014, the Applicant *Claus*, (*supra* para. 80) had also sought relief for removal of all references on the ADB website and documents that she was in the Division—ERMF. She had, however, not referred to this relief in the documents filed by her later, including in the Addendum to the Application dated 18 June 2014.

The Tribunal held that there was "no good ground to grant the above request (of *Claus*) as all information including details of the case and decision of the Tribunal are published on the ADB website" in accordance with Rule 2 (*sic* Rule 22) of the rules of Procedure. It was also noted "that the Tribunal did not receive a request for anonymity from the Applicant" pursuant to Practice Direction No. 2 (para. 81).

It will also be relevant to note that in *Mr. H v. ADB, ADBAT Reports, Vol. X*, [Decision No. 108, Decided on 6 January 2017], the Tribunal held that "Although not requested, the Tribunal grants confidentiality in light of the particulars of the case."

However, normally either party or both parties request that confidentiality be kept as regards identification of the Applicant and the persons referred to in the pleadings. This was the position in *Ms. G (No. 2) v. ADB, ADBAT Reports, Vol. X*, [Decision No. 107, Decided on 19 August 2016 para. 2]. The Tribunal held that having considered the above question in line with Practice Direction No. 3, the requests were granted.

V.   Reservation of Application under Rule 6 (11) of the Procedure Rules

Reservation of Application — Rule 6 (11) provides:

> "11.   If it appears that an application is clearly irreceivable or devoid of all merit, the President may instruct the Executive Secretary to take no further action thereon until the next session of the Tribunal. The Tribunal shall then consider the application and may either adjudge that it be summarily dismissed as clearly irreceivable or devoid of all merit, or order that it should be proceeded with in the ordinary way."[62]

---

[62] This is already amended as stated in paras 12 and 13 of Rule 6 of the Rules of Procedure effective 10 February 2021.

In a recent case, *Mr. Ocampo v. ADB, ADBAT Reports, Vol. X*, [Decision No. 122, Decided on 28 February 2019] the brief facts were "that on 20 November 2018, the Applicant filed the present Application with the Tribunal challenging the decision of the Director General, Budget, Personnel, and Management Systems Department ('DG, BPMSD'), of the Bank, by letter dated 12 November 2018. In this letter the DG, BPMSD, dismissed the allegations made by the Applicant on 12 October 2018 regarding abuse of discretion and breaches of confidentiality on the part of a Bank employee in her exchanges with the Bank's medical insurance provider ('the Provider'). The Director General held that the employee's actions were part of the normal course of the employee's official duties. The Application did not provide details regarding exhaustion of all other remedies available to current and former Bank employees. The Applicant, who was self-represented, sought US$400,000 for the psychological and moral damage allegedly suffered."

The Applicant joined the Bank on 10 January 1977 and took early retirement on 28 April 1997. Following an operation in late 2012 the Applicant experienced difficulties with the Provider regarding some claims. The Applicant had some correspondence with the DG, BPMSD, complaining, inter alia, of the poor performance of the Provider, and against Ms. X, an officer of BPMSD. The DG, BPMSD had in his letter dated 12 November 2018, written to the Applicant that the Bank *"had once again reviewed the documents you submitted involving [Ms. X] and reiterate our findings ..... we will no longer engage in any further correspondence with you on the matter."*

Concurrent with his correspondence with DG, BPMSD, on 6 October 2018 the Applicant first submitted a letter-memorandum to the Tribunal with the caption "Subject: Appeal for Restitution." Pursuant to Rule 6(9) of the Rules of Procedure this letter-memorandum was returned on 10 October 2018 by the Tribunal's Executive Secretary for noncompliance with the Rules, including for failure to exhaust all other remedies available within the Bank. A subsequent memorandum dated 12 November 2018 was likewise returned on 19 November 2018 for similar reasons. On 20 November 2018, the Applicant again submitted a memorandum to the Tribunal. This memorandum likewise was not in proper form as it provided no description of remedies exhausted within the Bank, but on 28 November 2018 the Tribunal advised the Applicant, copying the Bank, that with corrections, it would consider the Application. On 5 January 2019, the President of the Tribunal instructed the Executive Secretary to place the matter 9 before the Tribunal at its next session for consideration in accordance with Rule 6, paragraph 11 of the Procedure Rules.

The Tribunal after examining the facts in the case, came to the conclusion that the Applicant did not utilize the internal appeals mechanism of the Bank, as also pointed out by the Tribunal's Executive Secretary, when returning the earlier communications to him. It was noted that "[t]he case file also does not show that the President of the Bank has agreed to submit the Application directly to the Tribunal." (see *Jianming Xu v. ADB, ADBAT Reports, Vol. VII*, [Decision No. 69, Decided on 20 January 2005]. The exhaustion of internal remedies, must occur within the prescribed time limits. (See *Rive*, Decision No. 44 [1999], V ADBAT Reports 15, para. 9.)

The Tribunal therefore, concluded that it had no jurisdiction to entertain the Applicant's claim and that <u>the Application must, in accordance with paragraph 11 of Rule 6, be dismissed summarily</u>, as clearly irreceivable, (*emphasis added*) along with the claim for damages.

VI.   Punitive / *Ex Gratia* / Moral Damages

It may be mentioned that the ADBAT Statute does not provide specifically for (i) punitive damages, or (ii) *ex-gratia*/moral damages. However, there have been some exceptional circumstances where the Tribunal has dealt with such types of relief.

In *Cynthia M. Bares and Ors v. ADB, ADBAT Reports, Vol. I*, [Decision No. 5, Decided on 31 March 1995], the Tribunal dealt with a tragic case arising out of the homicide of the Bank's Assistant General Counsel, Mr. Robert E. Bares on 7 January 1992, committed on the premises of the Bank in Manila by a person employed as a security guard there. The action was brought against the Bank by Mrs. Cynthia Bares, widow of the deceased, her two children, and the Estate of the deceased. The proceedings were commenced by an Application 10 filed directly with the Tribunal on 4 June 1993, as agreed to by the Bank, under Article 11, paragraph 3 (a) of the Statute of the Tribunal.

The Applicants had received certain amounts under a life insurance policy, accidental death and dismemberment policy the cost of which was borne entirely by the Bank, as well as severance pay and workmen's compensation amounting to US$791,279.76. In addition, the Applicants became entitled to survivor's benefits under the Bank's retirement plan. The total of the various benefits may thus, over time, have yielded US$6,240,544.76, to the Applicants.

Mrs. Bares also claimed from the Bank US$4,220,346 by way of damages in respect of the alleged liability of the Bank for the tort committed against her husband. It did not take into account the payments to which the Applicants were entitled as mentioned in para. 28 above. The Applicants also sought "moral damages" as well as attorney's fees and costs. The Bank rejected these claims.

The Tribunal after careful consideration of the many arguments advanced on behalf of the Applicants, came to the conclusion that the liability of the Bank had to be assessed exclusively in terms of the contractual relationship between Mr. Bares and the Bank, and not in terms of obligations in tort or considerations of vicarious liability. For these reasons the Tribunal unanimously decided to dismiss the Application "in its entirety" but added the following:

RIDER

"The extraordinary circumstances of the death of Mr. Bares have inevitably added greatly to the dreadful distress and sense of loss felt by his family. The present decision leaves the family in the same financial position as if Mr. Bares had died otherwise than by the hand of one of the Bank's own security guards deliberately acting in breach of his duties within the very premises of the Bank. Notwithstanding the fact that no amount of money can diminish the sorrow of the family, the situation may be one in which the Bank will wish to consider the payment ex gratia to the family of Mr. Bares of a sum that may serve to demonstrate the Bank's sensitivity to the effect upon the family of the specially disturbing circumstances of the crime."

In other words, finally, the Tribunal nudged the bank to consider an *ex-gratia* payment of an amount to the family of Mr. Bares, stopping short of an order to pay the amount as a "remedy," which presumably the bank would have dealt with favorably. In the circumstances of the case, the Tribunal's suggestion to the bank to consider an *ex-gratia* payment to the Applicants, appears to be justified, though not specifically provided in the Statute.

In another case, *Ms. G v. ADB, ADBAT Reports, Vol. X* [Decision No. 106, Decided on 23 September 2015], the Applicant had questioned her performance assessment rating for 2013 Personal Review (PR) process and argued that the Respondent's comments on her performance had downplayed her capacity and accomplishments without supporting evidence. The Applicant also asserted that the performance review was motivated by improper purpose and completed in breach of due process. She also argued that the Respondent had breached procedures by not allowing her access to the assessments of her input supervisors. The Applicant had *inter alia* prayed for grant of reasonable costs and "other reliefs, just and equitable under the premises."

The Respondent argued that the Applicant's PR followed proper procedures and was not a decision that was arbitrary, discriminatory, improperly motivated, or adopted without due process.

The Tribunal noted however, that the "Respondent appeared not to have been fully faithful to the spirit of its implementing Guidelines and its memo" issued by BPMSD on 22 November 2013 in terms of citing the importance of (i) "face to face performance discussions," and "(ii) supervisors providing more extensive and valuable feedback." The Appeals Committee Report also mentioned reservations. In addition, it was noted that the Applicant was informed of the identity of only one of the three input supervisors consulted by the supervisor during the PR. The Tribunal noted that "[w]hile this was not a flaw in these circumstances it fell short of what was contemplated if not required by the Performance Management Implementation Guidelines."

Further, it was noted by the Tribunal that guidelines or tips are not mandatory, and their simple breach cannot be breach of due process. However, the failure to provide the Applicant with the names of all of her input supervisors on the Applicant's PR form and the fact that she did not become aware of the two further input supervisors until the end of the process were "to her disadvantage, lacked transparency and not in the full spirit of the PR."

The Tribunal came to the conclusion that the Applicant had failed to discharge her burden of proving that the Respondent had breached due process or acted arbitrarily or with improper motive. Nonetheless, the Tribunal held that it "believes that the Respondent could have taken more care to act in the spirit of its own PR Guidelines and Tips." In these circumstances, while the Applicant's other claims were dismissed, it "recommended" / ordered that the Applicant be given an *ex-gratia* payment of $5,000 by the Respondent bank.

VII.   Intangible Injury and Equitable Compensation

In some cases, the Tribunal concluded that the Applicant's claim is well founded in part. Although the Applicant may not be able to prove procedural unfairness and lack of due process because of discrimination or procedural flaw to vitiate the impugned decision, the Tribunal nevertheless concluded that the managerial style of the Respondent did cause some "intangible injury" to the Applicant, for which the Tribunal deems it appropriate for the bank to provide some equitable compensation.

In *Mr. E v. ADB, ADBAT Reports, Vol. X*, [Decision No. 103, Decided on 12 February 2014], the Applicant, a former employee of the Bank, claimed *inter alia* that he was severely harassed by three named supervisors. He claimed further that he was the victim of abuse of discretionary power exercised by the Respondent. He sought (a) disciplinary action against the alleged harassers; (b) substantial compensation; and (c) nullification of his six months' job duration with the Respondent.

After examining the process adopted by the Respondent in examining the complaint of harassment, the Tribunal stated that it is satisfied that the Respondent's assessment of the evidence overall did not involve any abuse of its discretionary power. Further, the Tribunal was satisfied that the Respondent followed all the procedural proprieties in dealing with the Applicant's formal complaint.

The other issue concerned not allowing the Applicant to attend an induction program on 31 May and 18 August 2001, invitations to which he had passed on to his supervisors. The Tribunal held that the failure to respond to the Applicant's e-mails on this issue "was a personnel practice that lacked transparency and was not fair to the Applicant," and was in breach of para. 2.1 of Administrative Order

(AO) 2.02 which requires ADB to be "guided by fair, impartial and transparent personnel ..... practices in the management of all its staff."

In conclusion the Tribunal held:

> "84. The Tribunal has found that the Applicant's claim is well-founded in part. The primary remedy envisaged by Article 10 of the ADBAT Statute is rescission of a contested decision or specific performance of an obligation invoked, with the fixing of compensation to be paid by the Bank if it declines to accept rescission or specific performance. However, in the circumstances of the present case the Tribunal considers that rescission or specific performance would be impractical and inappropriate. The Tribunal also considers that two of the three remedies requested by the Applicant — disciplinary action against the three supervisors and nullification of the Applicant's job duration with the Respondent — are either inappropriate or not within the Tribunal's powers. Nonetheless, it is reasonable to conclude that the Applicant suffered intangible injury as a result of the Respondent's breach of AO 2.11 and AO 2.02. For this he should be compensated. (*emphasis added*) (*See Alexander*, Decision No. 40 [1998] IV ADBAT Reports 41, para. 88, and Rive, Decision No. 44 [1999] V ADBAT Reports 15, para. 23)."

> "85. As regards the amount of compensation, there are two considerations which pull in opposite directions. On the one hand, the issue of the six month performance review reveals a weakness in the Applicant's case, which could depress the amount of compensation. But for the Applicant's resignation, as an inadequately performing probationer, he could have been terminated, in the absence of improvement in performance, from the end of the one month period envisaged in the performance review. On the other hand, the Country Director demonstrated inadequate support for the Applicant after his informal complaint of harassment on 9 May 2011, contrary to AO 2.11 and the supervisors' failure to respond to his reasonable request for their advice over induction programs breached both AO 2.11 and AO 2.02. The Application referred to 'mental trauma' and being 'tortured' by the supervisors. While such language is overly dramatic, it is likely that the Applicant suffered intangible loss as a result of the Respondent's breach of its own procedures. Pragmatically balancing these two considerations, the Tribunal will award equitable compensation of US $6,000."

> The other claims were dismissed.

The Tribunal did not order disciplinary action against the three supervisors, who the Applicant alleged had harassed him. The Tribunal, however, concluded that the concerned officers of the Respondent bank had committed breach of its own procedures, laid down in the relevant administrative orders, for which equitable compensation was awarded to the Applicant. It was up to the management of the Respondent bank to take any further action in the matter, taking into account the conclusions of the Tribunal, referred to above in para. 41 (*supra*).

Almost exactly a year later, the Tribunal dealt with a similar situation in *Claus v. ADB, ADBAT Reports, Vol. X*, [Decision No. 105, Decided on 13 February 2015].

In this case, the Applicant was a Senior Economist Level 5 of the Bank who challenged five decisions taken by the Respondent. Among those was her lateral transfer without consent from the Office of the Chief Economist (EROD) to Macroeconomics and Finance Research Division (ERMF) with effect from 1 January 2013. In the Application to the Tribunal, the Applicant had alleged that her transfer to ERMF breached the fundamental and essential terms of her contract and required her consent. One of her contentions was that when she was recruited to EROD, the Bank had represented that she would be reporting directly to the Bank's Chief Economist (CE) undertaking a special type of work. According to her, the job she was ultimately forced to transfer to in ERMF bore no resemblance to the job description she had been offered, including reporting to the Assistant Chief Economist (ACE) instead of the CE.

The Respondent argued that the above two positions in EROD and ERMF were essentially similar and thus, the Applicant's transfer from one to the other did not involve a demotion. While there was some difference in the scope of the research work required, the research focus of both positions was on macroeconomics and protection against shocks, further that the two positions overlapped very substantially. The Respondent acknowledged that the one main difference was that the EROD position involved reporting to the CE, while the ERMF position involved reporting to the ACE. However, the Respondent argued that a Senior Economist Level 5 in either position would have precisely the same status and seniority.

The Tribunal dealt with the reasons for the transfer of the Applicant from EROD to ERMF. It noted that "the advertised post for which the Applicant applied, which in effect contained the job description, indicated under the heading of 'Immediate Reporting Relationships' that the position would report to the Chief Economist. Yet after her transfer to ERMF the Applicant was to report to ACE rather than the CE. <u>This may not have been a demotion as such, but nevertheless was a significant change in her position</u>" (*emphasis added*). The Tribunal further noted that:

> "59. Taking into account the entirety of the circumstances as described above, including in particular, the significant change in the Applicant's reporting line, we find substance in the Applicant's claim that the Bank's action contravened AO 2.02, paragraph 2.1 <u>whereby ADB 'is guided by fair, impartial and transparent personnel policies and practices in the management of all its staff.'</u> This is enough to

justify an order of equitable compensation to be paid to the Applicant" (*emphasis added*).

Finally, the Tribunal held:

Remedy

"83. In relation to Decision 1, the Tribunal finds that neither rescission nor specific performance as provided in Article X of the Tribunal's Statute would be appropriate in the present case. In all the circumstances, it would be in order to award the Applicant some reasonable equitable compensation for intangible injury caused to the Applicant by the Respondent's action (see *Alexander*, Decision No. 40 [1998] IV ADBAT Reports and *Rive*, Decision No. 44 [1999] Volume V, ADBAT Reports)."

The Tribunal unanimously decided that the intangible injury suffered by the Applicant as a consequence of the bank's "breach of its own procedures will result in the Tribunal awarding equitable compensation" of $35,000 and $5,000 for reasonable costs incurred by the Applicant.

In four judgments delivered by the Tribunal on 2 October 2018, the Applicants had been proceeded against for misconduct, with regard to the purchases of tax-exempt vehicles. In these four cases—all reported in ADBAT Reports, Vol. X, namely, (i) *Ms. J v. ADB* [Decision No. 116]; (ii) *Mr. K v. ADB* [Decision No. 117]; (iii) *Ms. L v. ADB* [Decision No. 118]; and (iv) *Ms. M v. ADB* [Decision No. 119]—the Applicant had challenged the sanctions imposed on them, including dismissal for misconduct. In all four cases, the Tribunal held that the Applicants' claims failed, but also awarded $10,000 in damages to each of them for "intangible injury" and varying amounts as attorneys' fees.

In all of the above four cases, the Tribunal found that the Applicants' claims failed, but found that they had sustained intangible injury in relation to the Respondent's breach of AO 2.06, regarding excessive delay in the Appeal Committee's report and irregularities in signatures.

It will be sufficient to refer to the observations of the Tribunal in one of the aforesaid cases, that is, *Mr. K v. ADB* (*supra*), for awarding compensation for intangible injury.

Finding: Delay in issuing AC report

"67. The Tribunal notes that AO 2.06 of 19 February 2013 provides that the Appeals Committee is to submit its report to the President within 90 days of its receipt of the appeal (AO No. 2.06, para. 14). The Appeals Committee Rules of Procedure ('AC RoP') annexed to the AO define '*time limit*' as '*the time period within which an action has to be taken*' (AO 2.06, para. 1.2(h)). The statement in the cover memorandum to the AC report, that the 90-day time frame is '*indicated*' in AO 2.06, downplayed the definition of the time-limit in para. 1.2(h) of the AC RoP as a period in which an action '*has to be taken*.' The AC may '*at any stage of the proceedings*' 'extend any time limit which may apply under the Rules, taking into account the nature and complexity of the appeal' (AC RoP, para. 1.4(c)). However, nothing on the record indicates that the AC explicitly took that step or informed the parties that it was doing so."

"68. The AC's competence when reviewing decisions and disciplinary matters is essentially to determine whether ADB's Staff Regulations, Administrative Orders and policies and procedures have been correctly applied (AO 2.06, para. 9.2(d)). The AC thus does not conduct an independent investigation. It can hold hearings, which it did not do in this case, as well as request additional documentation, which it did in February and May 2017. According to the AC report, the last information it received was a memorandum from BPMSD on 26 May 2017, following the AC's request of 23 May 2017. It is not clear why it had taken this long for the AC to request this information, or whether or not a copy of this memorandum was provided to the Applicant for possible comment."

"69. In explaining the reasons for failing to submit the report within the stipulated period, the AC referred to '*the intricacies of the case*' and the amount of documentation, including additionally requested information, and the time necessary to consider the appeal. The appeal was complex, justifying in the Tribunal's view a possible extension by the AC of the time limit, in order to grasp the relevant elements of the four cases, as permitted by its rules. But in the eyes of the Tribunal, the delay — exceeding by almost four times the normal time limit of 90 days — was excessive. In the interest of transparency, the AC, while it might not be required to do so, should also have informed the parties of the new time limit it was providing for itself under para. 1.4(c) of its RoP" (*emphasis added*).

(b) Signatures on the AC report

"70. The Tribunal calls attention to two noteworthy features of the signatures on the final page of the AC report. In one case, one member signed 'for' another member, and in the other case the Secretary of the AC signed 'for' a third AC member."

Finding: Signatures on the AC report

"71. The Tribunal finds it questionable that these signatures were made without an indication of authorization to the person signing, particularly given the lack of unanimity in respect of some conclusions of the AC and the serious sanctions imposed on the Applicant. While the Tribunal does not conclude that the shortcoming was of sufficient import to invalidate the AC's report, it expresses concern that the Bank has not taken greater care in this respect."

Compensation

"72. With regard to the excessive delay in the AC report and the irregularities in signature, the Tribunal finds that, while they did not affect the outcome and thus did not amount to a denial of due process as a whole, the deviation by the Appeals Committee from its own rules warrants an award of some compensation to the Applicant for intangible injury" (*emphasis added*).

It is relevant to refer to the observations of the Tribunal in an earlier case, decided more than 22 years before the cases mentioned in para. 48 (*supra*), namely, *Latif M. Chaudhry v. ADB, ADBAT Reports, Vol. II*, [Decision No. 23, Decided on 13 August 1996]. In this case the Tribunal had also awarded equitable compensation, on the grounds that the Respondent did not follow proper procedure "carefully." Here, the Respondent, after conducting a preliminary investigation into the matter, based on the facts, concluded that there were possible grounds for discipline, on some phone calls made by the Applicant. The Respondent appointed a Committee of Inquiry (COI) to find facts and make recommendations to the President of the bank.

The Applicant claimed that the inquiry process was flawed and claimed damages in excess of $1 million, which was refused by the bank and challenged before the Tribunal.

The Tribunal concluded that at least until acted upon by the ADB President, the 7 March Report and the 10 March observations of the COI were properly treated as internal documents intended for the purpose of advising and making recommendations to the President.

It was held:

"Once the President communicated his formal decision that no disciplinary measures should be imposed, A.O. No. 2.08 appears to contemplate that the two pertinent COI documents should have been made available to the Applicant, upon request, with reasonable promptness." The Reports were ultimately given to the Applicant's counsel, after his repeated requests well before he filed a claim with the concerned officer of the Bank and then his appeal to the Appeals Committee. In these circumstances, the Tribunal stated that "Nonetheless, the delay of more than two months was unnecessarily long, even if the Applicant can point to no precise injury that resulted from such delay."

The Tribunal concluded:

> "45. In sum, almost all of the Applicant's contentions must be rejected. There were some respects in which proper procedure was not carefully followed, in particular with regard to the breach of confidentiality of the disciplinary proceedings and the delayed disclosure of the COI Report and Observations. In these latter respects, <u>it is likely that some intangible injury was caused to the Applicant;</u> <u>the extent of that impact cannot be precisely measured, although it</u> <u>is clear to the Tribunal that it did not rise to the level of warranting a</u> <u>significant compensatory judgment</u>. The Tribunal considers an award of US$5,000 to be equitable. Although the Applicant has requested that the Respondent be directed to pay his costs, the Tribunal notes that it would ordinarily be appropriate to make such an award taking into account the proportion of his claims that were ultimately sustained of the pleadings and annexes proffered by the Applicant, his claims for costs should be denied" (*emphasis added*).

From the above decisions it can be stated that where the Tribunal find that the Respondent bank's, officers have breached "its own procedure," for example AO 2.02, which requires it to be "guided by fair, impartial and transparent personnel ..... practices in the management of all its staff," it may come to the conclusion that the Applicant has suffered "intangible injury" and award some "equitable compensation" to the Applicant, while dismissing the other claims.

VIII. Legal Fees and Costs

Under Article X, para. 2 of the Statute, the Tribunal can award "reasonable costs" incurred by the Applicant's counsel in the claim before the Tribunal.

In *Perrin et al. (No. 3) v. ADB, ADBAT Reports, Vol. X* [Decision No. 113, Decided on 21 July 2018], in the Further Reply, the Applicants "again" requested an award for reasonable legal costs incurred by them, [in accordance with Article X(2) of the Statute], taking into account "the nature and complexity of the case and the nature and quality of the work performed." The Applicants were denied their requests for reimbursement of legal and other expenses in *Perrin et al. v. ADB, ADBAT Reports, Vol. X* [Decision No. 109, Decided on 6 May 2017] and in *Perrin et al. (No. 2) v. ADB, ADBAT Reports, Vol X,* [Decision No. 112, Decided on 28 February 2018], where it was stated that the decision on the matter relating to costs was deferred until resolution on the merits.

In *Perrin et al. (No. 3) v. ADB, (supra)* the Tribunal held:

> "106. It is settled jurisprudence that this Tribunal may award reasonable legal fees and costs pursuant to Article X (2) of the ADBAT Statute, (see text in Para 6, *supra*).

In addition, proof of costs must be provided:

From its inception (Lindsey, Decision No. 1 [1992]. I ADBAT Reports), the Tribunal has stressed that an Applicant's Reply must contain proof of his costs. (Galang, Decision No. 55 [2002], VI ADBAT Reports, para. 50)" The Tribunal noted that only part of costs had been provided.

"107. The Tribunal has also noted that although an Applicant may succeed only in part, where issues raised are of importance the Tribunal has considered it equitable to award costs:

> 'Although the Applicants have not succeeded on the merits, their pleadings nonetheless were very useful to the tribunal on issues that were important and complex, and the Applicants did prevail with regard to the preliminary objections. Accordingly, the Tribunal decides to award a sum towards their costs.' (*Mesch and Siy* (No. 4), Decision No. 35 [1997], III ADBAT Reports, para 351. See also *De Armas et al.*, Decision No. 39 [1998], IV ADBAT Reports, para. 93.)"

"108. The Tribunal deems it totally proper and important that staff have the possibility to challenge the legality of changes to underlying general rules that apply or may apply to many present and future staff. The Applicants and the Respondent agreed to submit the case directly to the Tribunal in order to obtain a ruling on the legality of the measures in the interest of legal certainty. Accordingly, the Respondent initially did not raise preliminary objections."

"109. Having considered the representation of the parties, the criteria set out in Article X (2), and the Tribunal's jurisprudence, the Tribunal considers that the Applicants have raised a significant issue in law that had the potential to affect a much wider group of staff regarding their fundamental and essential rights."

"110. It must at the same time be underlined, as the history of the present case shows, that some of the costs were avoidable. Time and resources were lost following inadequate preparation and presentation of the applications. Moreover, the Tribunal notes that the Applicants' pleadings were assisted in great part by the Respondent's voluntary provision of relevant documentation in support of their claims. The Tribunal considers that under these circumstances an amount of US$10,000 is a fair contribution towards costs."

The 36 Applicants had requested an award for "reasonable legal costs" incurred by them. In *Perrin et al.* (No. 3) (*supra*), although the Tribunal unanimously decided to dismiss the Applicants' claims, they nevertheless awarded some costs to the Applicants, which decision had been deferred in Decision No. 112, until resolution on the merits.

IX.   Remand of the Case

Article X, para. 3, (see text para. 6, supra) provides that at the request of the President of the bank, and before the determination of the merits, the Tribunal may order the case to be remanded for compliance with the required procedure.

This is a situation where the Tribunal remands the case to correct procedural errors before the case is decided on the merits. The above provision does not appear to have been resorted to so far; and after the further decision is taken by the bank, that can also be challenged before the Tribunal, under Article 11 of the Statute.

X.   Finality of the Order

Under Article X, para. 4 (see text in para. 6 above), the compensation and reasonable costs ordered by the Tribunal under paras. 1 and 2 of the Article "shall be paid by the Bank," meaning that it is final and there is no appeal.

XI.   Compensation to Be Paid by the Applicant to the Bank

Article X, para. 6 of the Statute provides:

> "6. The Tribunal may order reasonable compensation to be made by the Applicant to the Bank for all or part of the cost of defending the case, if it finds that:
>
> > (a)   the application was manifestly without foundation either in fact or under existing law, unless the Applicant demonstrates that the application was based on a good faith argument for an extension, modification, or reversal or existing law; or
> >
> > (b)   the Applicant intended to delay the resolution of the case or to harass the Bank or any of its officers or employees.
>
> The amount awarded by the Tribunal shall be collected by way of deductions from payments owed by the Bank to the Applicant or otherwise, as determined by the President of the Bank. For the purpose of this paragraph, payments due to the Applicant under the

Staff Retirement Plan shall not be deemed to be payments owed by the Bank to the Applicant."[63]

Article X (6) (b) of the ADBAT Statute was considered by the Tribunal in *Mr. H v. ADB, ADBAT Reports, Vol. X*, [Decision No. 108, Decided on 6 January 2017]: Briefly stated, the relevant facts of this case were that the Applicant had applied for a higher position in ADB (the Respondent bank) but was unsuccessful. He challenged the selection process before the Appeals Committee which found that the selection decision was procedurally flawed. Prior to the Appeals Committee Report becoming known, the Applicant had filed a criminal complaint for "libel" and "grave slander" with the Philippines authorities against 10 ADB officers involved in the selection process.

According to the Applicant, the Screening Committee had "circulated to various departments across ADB" "highly defamatory language that maliciously maligned my reputation." He argued that in reporting the alleged crime, he was pursuing criminal justice rather than an employment grievance and the Philippines courts provided him the only forum for access to justice. The ADB President on being informed of the Applicant's filing a criminal complaint and on the first service of the subpoena on a bank official, summarily dismissed the Applicant. Three months after his dismissal, the bank imposed an additional sanction of discontinuing participation in the Post Retirement Group Medical Insurance Plan (PRGMIP) by the Applicant and his dependent family. In his Application to the Tribunal, the Applicant challenged his summary dismissal and the discontinuation of the insurance plan for him and his dependents.

In the case of *Mr. H* [Decision No. 108] (*supra*), the Respondent had pleaded that the Tribunal may order costs against the Applicant "for defending the case" in accordance with Article X para. 6(b) of the Statute. It was held:

> "98. The Tribunal does not find that the Applicant intended to harass the Bank or any of its officers or employees in bringing 'this case' to the Tribunal. It accordingly found that the conditions under Article X para. 6 (b) are not met and denies the Respondent's request for costs ....."

It will be interesting to recall that in one of the meetings of the Committee of Administrative Tribunal Matters held a few years back, during one of the sessions of the Tribunal, with some senior officers and representatives of the Staff Council of the bank, the Secretary of the Staff Council raised the issue about Article X, para. 6, regarding compensation to be made by the Applicant to the bank. The view of the Staff Council representative was that this provision is an unnecessary deterrent for an aggrieved employee, who wants to file an application in the Tribunal and that it should be deleted. However, it was explained by the

---

[63]   There is a similar provision (Article XV) in the Statute of the International Monetary Fund Administrative Tribunal (IMF AT); but no such provision in the Statute of the World Bank Administrative Tribunal (WBAT), 1980 as amended in 2001, 2009.

Members of the Tribunal that this provision has not been applied so far by the Tribunal against any Applicant. The Members of the Tribunal explained that this provision in the Statute will only be applied in a judicious manner, which allayed the fears of the staff members.

It may also be added that the Tribunal has not invoked the provisions of Article X para. 6 in the past 30 years, to award cost to the Respondent for defending a case against an Applicant. The provision will act as a deterrent to the Applicant to pursue a frivolous case, which has no legal merit, but such cases will indeed be very rare. Further, the provision will not deter an application "based on a good faith argument" or was not intended to delay the resolution of the case or harass the bank or any of its officers or employees. This was also clearly referred to in the Decision in *Mr. H* (*supra*).

XII. Immunities of the Bank and Bank Staff Filing Criminal Complaint or Civil Suit in National Courts

As already mentioned above, any "member of the staff" of the bank, as defined in Article II para. 2, who alleges nonobservance of the contract of employment or terms of appointment, can file an application before the Tribunal for the remedies as prescribed in Article X. It is also clear that the Tribunal alone has jurisdiction to settle such matters involving disputes between the Applicants, who are current or former members of the bank staff.

However, recently, in a series of cases, from January 2017 to July 2018, the Applicants, who were all ADB staff members, had filed either a criminal complaint before the local authorities against the bank and some bank officials or filed a civil suit against the bank for compensation, in the legal system of another country. This was in **addition** to the Applicants filing Applications before the Tribunal for seeking the reliefs as provided in the Statute.

One of the cases is *Mr. H v. ADB, ADBAT Reports, Vol. X,* [Decision No. 108, Decided on 6 January 2017]. The brief facts were that the Applicant joined the bank on 21 November 1994, and from 27 May 2014 served as a Level 8 Senior Advisor within the Office of the Director General, Central and West Asia Department.

On 5 January 2015, the Applicant applied for the Level 7/8/9 position in the Regional and Sustainable Development Department (RSDD) but was unsuccessful. He challenged the selection process before the Appeals Committee. The Appeals Committee found the selection decision was procedurally flawed with "inaccurate statements about the [Applicant's] professional experience" having been entered into the official record. Prior to the Appeals Committee Report becoming known, the Applicant filed a criminal complaint for "libel" and "grave slander" with the Philippines authorities against 10 ADB officers involved in the selection process. He alleged that the Vice President (VP) Panel Notes prepared by the Screening Committee and "circulated to various departments across ADB" "included highly defamatory language that maliciously maligned my reputation." He argued that in reporting the alleged crime, he was pursuing criminal justice rather than an employment grievance and that the Philippine courts provided his only forum for access to justice. The President of the bank, on being informed of the Applicant's filing of the criminal complaint and on the first service of the subpoena on a bank official, summarily dismissed the Applicant. Three months after his dismissal, the bank imposed the additional sanction of discontinuing participation in the Post-Retirement Group Medical Insurance Plan by the Applicant and his dependent family. The application before the Tribunal related to two matters: (i) his summary dismissal, and (ii) the discontinuation of the insurance.

The Tribunal, after considering the relevant provisions of AO 2.04 "Disciplinary Measures and Procedures," came to the conclusion that the "crime," according to the Applicant, was committed in the framework of the selection process. It was held:

> "67. ….. In this context, the Tribunal also recalls the Appeals Committee's decision to uphold the Appeal was based on the shortcomings in the procedures and not on the contents of the statements made by the officials in the selection process. The statements were made in the process of the selection procedure and, therefore, it was in an official capacity for which <u>the persons are protected by the immunities that the Bank enjoys. These immunities are essential to the functioning of international organisations such as the ADB and well recognized by international law. It is for the Bank to decide whether or not it will waive these immunities in specific circumstances</u>" (*emphasis added*).

It was further observed that "the Tribunal considers that the filing of a criminal complaint against ADB and/or members of the ADB management team or staff in the national legal system is 'a grave issue' for an international institution, particularly as the Applicant's grievance had not yet been resolved within the internal justice system." This was a violation of a staff member's duties and responsibilities to ADB under Administrative Order (AO) 2.02, para. 4.3 (iii), which provides that the claims of staff members concerning the terms and conditions of their employment have *"a right of appeal to ADB's Administrative Tribunal. Staff members who have such claims and had access to the foregoing procedures may not resort to national courts or other tribunals outside ADB to resolve such claims."*

The Applicant had contended that the filing of the criminal complaint was simply for reporting a "crime." The Tribunal observed that the Applicant had an opportunity to avail of the ADB's internal justice system, namely reporting an alleged crime under the Integrity Principles and Guidelines to the Office of Anticorruption and Integrity (OAI). If he was still not satisfied, he could have asked the bank to waive the officers' protection of immunity, which he had failed to do before taking legal action in the local courts.

The Tribunal noted that the Applicant sought monetary damages amounting to ₱50 million (approximately $1 million at the end of 2017) from his colleagues when making the criminal complaint, which provided "evidence that he was motivated to achieve more than merely reporting a crime." The Tribunal also noted that in this case, the facts were not in doubt, the criminal complaint had been filed, and a subpoena issued. Harm had already been inflicted upon the bank, as well as the accused persons, which led to the dismissal decision. Therefore, the Tribunal concluded that the Applicant's initiation of the criminal proceedings before the Mandaluyong City Prosecutor constituted "serious misconduct" contemplated by AO 2.04. The Tribunal further concluded that the decision of the President of the bank to summarily dismiss him on this ground was neither discriminatory, nor an abuse of discretion, nor retaliatory.

The Tribunal further held in para. 88 of Decision No. 108 that "AO 2.04 para. 6.3 further provides '*dismissal for misconduct is also appropriate when the breach of trust is so serious that continuation of the staff member's service is not in the interest of the Bank.*'" The filing of the criminal complaint was a clear breach, with serious adverse consequences for the bank and his colleagues; and it was deliberate, hence the personal circumstances and length of service of the Applicant were also taken into account. Moreover, it was held that "... each of these elements justify a finding under para. 6.3 that the breach of trust was so serious that continuation of the Applicant's service was not in the interest of the Bank" (*emphasis added*).

Therefore, the Tribunal concluded that the summary dismissal of the Applicant was proportionate to the misconduct and was valid. As he had "lost his core argument," the Tribunal dismissed all other claims, except rescinding the additional disciplinary measure of discontinuing medical insurance plan, and granted him the cost of $1,000.

Just four months later, in *Maria Lourdes Drilon v. ADB, ADBAT Reports, Vol. X,* [Decision No. 110, Decided on 6 May 2017], the Tribunal decided a similar case where the Applicant had filed a criminal complaint with the local authorities. The Applicant contested the decision of the bank, before the Tribunal, to terminate her service as a Senior Natural Resource Economist International Staff at Level 5, for unsatisfactory performance communicated to her on 23 November 2015.

While the internal grievance procedure was continuing, on 29 January 2016, the Applicant filed a criminal complaint against eight of her former bank colleagues, including her supervisor, alleging "cyber libel" for posting her written assessment onto ADB's internal IT system. The Respondent explained that this assessment was not made public. The criminal complaint was dismissed on 27 May 2016 "by virtue of the immunities afforded to the ADB," but a motion for reconsideration with the Prosecutor's Office was pending on the date the Tribunal gave its judgment on 6 May 2017.

The Tribunal, following the findings in *Mr. H* [Decision No. 108] (para. 71, *supra*), held "that a legitimate or *bona fide* discharge of the official duties by Bank officials in the assessment of the Applicant's performance in accordance with the Bank's rules and procedures cannot be construed as 'criminal conduct'" (*emphasis added*). The Tribunal, therefore, disagreed with the Applicant's statement that her employment claims before the Tribunal and her criminal complaint were distinct.

It was further held by the Tribunal (para. 74 of Decision No. 110) that it disagreed with the Applicant's statement that her employment claims before the Tribunal and the criminal complaint were distinct. Further it was held that "[f]or a former senior and experienced Bank official to have taken such action with the local authorities was incompatible with the system of internal review which is linked to the immunities from jurisdiction enjoyed by the ADB pursuant to agreement with the Government of the Philippines." The Tribunal, therefore, unanimously dismissed all the reliefs claimed by the Applicant, including costs.

In the third case of *Mr. I v. ADB, ADBAT Reports, Vol. X* [Decision No. 114, Decided on 21 July 2018], the Applicant, an International Staff member, challenged the decision of the Respondent bank to terminate his employment on 14 December 2016. His last date of employment was 4 May 2017, under the 2016 Early Separation Program. The Applicant contested the 28 August 2017 decision of the President of the bank to accept the recommendation of the Appeals Committee to terminate his appointment "in the interest of good administration," in accordance with AO 2.05 (Termination Policy) para. 8.1.

The Applicant first filed his application in the Tribunal on 14 November 2017, and later, on 27 November 2017, which was received in the Tribunal on 4 December 2017. The pleadings in the case were completed on 16 April 2018.

Meanwhile, on 5 June 2017, one month and one day after his last date of employment, the Applicant sent a letter to the bank threatening to take legal action in a national court against the President and members of the Review Panel in connection with the Applicant's termination of employment. Those named were accused of various criminal acts, including defamation and corruption, under the Criminal Code and Civil Code of Indonesia. The legal notice of accusations was copied to several institutions, including Indonesia's Minister of Finance, the House of Representatives of Indonesia, and various embassies in Indonesia.

The Respondent replied to the Applicant's letter on 19 June 2017 explaining the immunities enjoyed by its staff under its Charter and the internal dispute mechanisms available. Despite this, on 4 July 2017, the Applicant wrote again to the bank with the same threat; and on 2 January 2018, while this application was pending before the Tribunal, the Applicant commenced a civil action against the "Asian Development Bank in this case represented by its Senior Management" before the First Court of Central Jakarta. As part of his plea, the Applicant requested the court to punish the Respondent by ordering it to pay him $1 billion and to pay all court fees and costs.

When the Tribunal dealt with the relief as prayed for by the Applicant, it reiterated the earlier findings of the Tribunal in the *Drilon* case, [Decision No. 110, Decided on 6 May 2017 para. 74 (*supra*) that such action is incompatible with the immunities enjoyed by the bank; further, that this action constituted a "serious misconduct under A.O 2.04, and A.O 2.02, which precludes the Applicant from pursuing employment related grievances in a national legal system."

It was further held by the Tribunal that such immunities arose from the Agreement with the member States as provided in Article 55(i) of the Agreement Establishing the ADB. The Tribunal also noted that when the Applicant wrote to ADB on 5 June 2017 accusing the members of the Review Panel of criminal acts and threatening to take legal action, he copied it to several other 30 national governments via their embassies. This contradicted the terms of his appointment with the Bank as an international civil servant, and damaged the reputation of the Respondent. This Tribunal has exclusive jurisdiction to settle matters involving alleged nonobservance of staff members' terms of employment. For these reasons, the Tribunal has decided to take the Applicant's actions into account in deciding on relief (*emphasis added*).

In the final relief given by the Tribunal to the Applicant, the impugned decision of the President of the bank was rescinded on the ground of breach of due process by the second Review Panel. Pursuant to Article X, para. 1 of the Statute, the Tribunal fixed the compensation at $1,000, to be paid to the Applicant, should the President of the bank decide that the Applicant shall be compensated without further action being taken in the case; and to be paid the cost of $500. All other claims for relief were denied.

In another similar case, *Ma. Editha T. Cruz v. ADB, ADBAT Reports, Vol. X.* [Decision No. 115, Decided on 21 July 2018], decided by the Tribunal on the same date as *Mr. I* [Decision No. 114 (*supra*)], the Respondent had also decided to terminate the employment of the Applicant, under the same Early Separation Program (2016). However, pursuant to Article X, para. 1 of the Statute, the compensation fixed by the Tribunal in the *Cruz* case was a 12-month remuneration, should the President of the bank decide that no further action be taken in the case, together with costs of $8,000. Though the reliefs given in these two cases were similar, to the extent that the Applicants were ordered to be reinstated to their positions, the compensation amounts and costs awarded under Article X, para. 1 were different. As stated in *Mr. I* (Decision No. 114, para. 55), the Tribunal had taken into account the Applicant's action of filing a civil action against the bank in the national court and the immunities from jurisdiction enjoyed by the bank. In addition, the Tribunal's exclusive jurisdiction to settle such matters involving the alleged nonobservance of staff members' terms of employment, while granting the relief, which was far less in monetary terms compared with what was granted to Applicant *Cruz*.

It is clear from the above decisions that the Applicant can seek remedies relating to employment or service-related grievances against the bank only before the Administrative Tribunal, which has exclusive jurisdiction in the matter. In other words, bank staff cannot institute any criminal complaint or a civil suit in a national legal system, which is contrary to the provisions of the Agreement establishing ADB and amounts to "serious misconduct" under the bank's AO 2.04.

In conclusion, it may be stated that the Tribunal will take into account the action of the Applicant, while granting the remedies under Article X of the Statute, especially where it is in contravention with his/her terms of appointment with the bank, as an international civil servant or where the Applicant has pursued employment-related issues before any national legal system. If an ADB staff member has any grievance or dispute with the bank regarding his terms of employment or any other issues relating to his/her contract of employment with the bank, that person can file an application to the Tribunal for adjudication in the matter, as provided in Article 11 of the Statute. The Tribunal has exclusive jurisdiction in such matters and the decisions of the Tribunal are final and binding.

XIII. Remedy for Clarification of a Decision of the Tribunal

In several cases, the Tribunal has ordered specific performance under Article X of the Statute, and at the same time also fixed the amount of compensation to be paid to the Applicant, in the event the President of the bank decides to pay the compensation without taking further action in the case. The President of the bank, who has the authority to determine whether to implement that decision, or to pay the amount of compensation fixed by the Tribunal "[at] the same time" may decide to pay the compensation ordered. In some of these cases, the Applicants have filed another application before the Tribunal to seek clarification as to their entitlements. (See for example, *Anjum Ibrahim v. ADB, ADBAT Reports, Vol. VIII* [Decision No. 86B, Decided on 19 August 2009] and *Ms. Cruz (No. 2) v. ADB, ADBAT Reports, Vol. X* [Decision No. 121, Decided on 28 February 2019]).

In Decision No. 121 (*supra*) the Applicant questioned whether the Respondent in the earlier case, *Ma. Editha T. Cruz v. ADB, ADBAT Reports, Vol. X,* [Decision No. 115, Decided on 21 July 2018] had discretion not to reinstate an employee, even if the Tribunal had ordered it, and the employee was ready and willing to be reinitiated. The Tribunal clarified the position as follows:

> "20.   The 'further action' referred to in Article X, para. 1 means further action by the Bank, not — as the Applicant has argued — further action by the Tribunal. The Tribunal's interpretation of Article X, para. 1 of

the Statute is supported by the text submitted to and approved by the ADB Board of Directors when the Board endorsed the Statute of the Tribunal in 1991. This text stated, '*The judgement of the Administrative Tribunal would be binding on the Bank and without appeal. However, the Bank would have the option to pay compensation (as determined by the Tribunal) in instances where it decided that it would be against the Bank's best interests to comply with a decision requesting specific performance .....'*" [followed by illustrative examples].

It was further held in *Ms. Cruz (No. 2)* that:

"21.   In Decision No. 115 (*Ma. Editha T. Cruz v. ADB, ADBAT Reports, Vol. X,* [Decided on 21 July 2018]) the Tribunal ordered in part that the Applicant be reinstated to her position and be made whole for lost earnings (minus the separation package), plus interest. At the same time, it additionally fixed an amount of compensation to be paid to the Applicant 'should the President of the Bank decide that the Applicant shall be compensated without further action being taken in the case .....' As noted in Decision No. 86-B, the Tribunal's '*authority to order specific performance is limited by the second sentence of Article X, ... which reserves to the President of the Bank the authority to determine whether to implement that specific performance. The requirement that the Tribunal fix an amount of compensation 'at the same time' provides the basis for granting compensation in lieu of an order to take the further action to reinstate .....*' (Decision No. 86-B, *supra*, para 10). Thus when, 'in the interest of the Bank,' the President legitimately decides not to take the further action to reinstate, <u>the amount of compensation awarded to the individual concerned replaces an order of reinstatement</u>" (*emphasis added*).

Thus, the Tribunal clarified its "reinstatement" Decision No. 115, *inter alia*, stating that what the Applicant might have received as a voluntary participant in the Early Separation Program is irrelevant to what the Tribunal has awarded to her in that Decision. The Tribunal held "that a person cannot simultaneously receive a salary as an ADB staff member and a pension as a Bank retiree." Further, it was held that in implementing the Decision No. 115 and calculating the amount to be paid to the Applicant for all lost earnings, the bank took the relevant elements into account.

XIV. Remedy to Revise an Earlier Judgment

Another remedy which the Applicant in an earlier case can seek is revision of the judgment of the Tribunal under Article XI of the Statute, which provides:

Article XI

1.   A party to a case in which a judgment has been delivered may, in the event of the discovery of a fact which by its nature might have had a decisive influence on the judgment of the Tribunal and which at the time the judgment was delivered was unknown both to the Tribunal and to that party, request the Tribunal, within a period of six months after that party acquired knowledge of such fact, to revise the judgment.

2.   The request shall contain the information necessary to show that the conditions laid down in paragraph 1 of this Article have been complied with. It shall be accompanied by the original or a copy of all supporting documents.

For the first time, recently, an Applicant made a request to reopen two earlier judgments of the Tribunal, in *Ms. D (No. 3) v. ADB, ADBAT Reports, Vol. X* [Decision No. 111, Decided on 28 February 2018], namely (i) Decision No. 95 of 8 September 2011, and (ii) Decision No. 99 of 15 August 2012.

The Summary of Decision No. 95, 8 September 2011 is that in that case:

"5.   the Tribunal concluded that the Respondent had met the requirements of due process in evaluating the Applicant's performance at the end of her probationary period as set out in Administrative Order ('AO') 2.01, section 11. Accordingly, the Tribunal dismissed unanimously the Applicant's challenge to the Bank's decision not to confirm her employment as a National Officer of the ADB Resident Mission in China" on the grounds alleged by her.

Under those circumstances, the Tribunal concluded that there was no merit in the Applicant's claim that proper procedures had not been followed, or that the decision was arbitrary, pre-motivated, unjustified, or distorted.

Summary of Decision No. 99, [15 August 2012] was that on

17 March 2012, the Applicant made a request for review of Decision No. 95 on two grounds. First, she alleged that the Performance Development Plan (PDP) review procedure was not followed by the Country Director, People's Republic of China (CD, PRCM). Secondly, she alleged that the CD did not hold independent discussions with the three Task Managers who had worked with the Applicant.

The Tribunal concluded that the "Applicant essentially repeats the arguments already put forward before the Tribunal." The Tribunal also noted that as all judgments of the Tribunal are final, any decision to review a prior decision is to be "construed very strictly."

In her third request in this matter, *Ms. D* asked the Tribunal to

(i)   reopen her cases and review all evidence and facts to revise its decisions;

(ii)   remove all restrictions on her, including restrictions on her engagement in any ADB-administered projects or application for any ADB staff position; and

(iii) make appropriate financial compensation for damage to her career and persistent mental suffering.

According to Article IX, para. 1 of the Statute, "All decisions of the Tribunal ..... shall be final and binding." Article XI, para. 1 of the Statute provides one exception to the principle of finality of Tribunal judgments, whereby the Applicant can request the revision of a judgment, provided that three conditions are satisfied, namely:

(i)   discovery of a new fact,

(ii)   which at the time when the judgment was delivered was unknown both to the Tribunal and that party,

(iii) which by its nature might have had a decisive influence on the judgment.

(See also *Hua Du (No. 2) v. ADB, ADBAT Reports, Vol. VIII* [Decision No. 102, Decided on 31 July 2013].)

It was clearly noted in para. 41 of Decision No. 111 (*supra*), that the "jurisprudence of the Tribunal has been consistent in declining to review its earlier judgments where the Applicant fails to meet the conditions set out in Article XI. In particular, this Tribunal has refused a request for review where the Applicant fails to adduce a new and relevant fact that was not known to either the Tribunal or Applicant at the time of the judgment."

The Tribunal noted in para. 46 of *Ms. D v. ADB (No. 3)*, (*supra*) that:

> *Ms. D* essentially repeats the allegations that she has already made to the Tribunal in her application for review of Decision No. 95: that untrue information was provided by her CD that could be challenged successfully if oral evidence of her Task Managers were to be admitted; and that the PDP processes were not followed. In its Decision No. 95 and Decision No. 99, the Tribunal denied admission of additional oral evidence on the ground that Bank officials had properly considered other relevant evidence and material. In Decision No. 95, the Tribunal found that the Bank had conducted its PDP processes properly. As the Applicant had not produced any fact unknown to the Tribunal or the Applicant at the time of the judgment in Decision No. 95, that

by its nature might have had a decisive influence on that judgment, the request for revision was denied in Decision No. 99.

In the present case, it was again concluded that Ms. D has failed to satisfy the conditions for revision under Article XI. It was held "that Ms. D has failed to meet the conditions set by Article XI because she has not produced any fact that was unknown to her or the Tribunal at the time of the judgments in Decision No. 95 and Decision No. 99 that might decisively influence the outcomes of those judgments." It was further held:

> "50. This conclusion is consistent with the fundamental principle of the rule of law which is that of finality of judgements. <u>It is in the public interest to have certainty in law and judgements of the Tribunal are subject to revision only if other legal conditions are fulfilled</u>" (*emphasis added*).

Finally, the Tribunal unanimously denied the request of the Applicant *Ms. D* to reopen Decisions No. 95 and No. 99, and also denied her requests for relief.

The Revision Application cannot be used by the dissatisfied Applicant as if it is an "appeal;" if the Applicant is not satisfied with the judgment, he/she should ask for "revision" of the decision on the basis of the same facts and allegations made earlier, that some "mistakes" have occurred. There has to be discovery of a "new fact" presented, which was previously unknown to both the Tribunal and the party that would have had a decisive influence on the judgment. Additionally, the request to the Tribunal has to be made within a period of 6 months after that party acquired knowledge of such a fact to revise the judgment. The principles of finality and *res judicata* of the Tribunal judgments set out in the Statute (Article IX) are equally important. The exception carved out under Article XI to revise an earlier judgment can be exercised only if all the conditions laid down therein are fulfilled.

It may be added that so far, the Tribunal has not granted the relief of revision of an earlier delivered judgment, as the Applicants have failed to fulfill the legal requirements under Article XI of the Statute. These conditions have to be construed strictly as the finality of judgments is also a fundamental principle of the rule of law.

Finally, it may be useful to recollect what was stated in para. 5 above—that is, what the Applicant who has filed an application in the Tribunal is mainly concerned with is the final relief that is granted by the Tribunal. In this connection, a quick check of the reliefs granted may be done by the Tribunal, say in the last 20 applications filed and decided, that are reported in the ADBAT Reports, Volume X.

Only in one case was the application filed summarily dismissed [Decision No. 122]— the case of *Mr. Ocampo*—for noncompliance with the law under Article 11, para. 3(a) of the Statute. In another case [Decision No. 104], the application by *Mr. F* was dismissed on merits on the ground that the Applicant had not met the burden of proving any violations of the Respondent's obligation toward him. However, in this case, the Tribunal had commented that to use "pejorative terms" to describe the Applicant at a personal level by the Respondent, "does not assist the legal process or the Tribunal." In the *Drilon case* [Decision No. 110], the Tribunal had denied the relief on merits as the Applicant had failed to discharge her burden of proof. In another case [Decision No. 120], where both the Applicant and the Respondent had requested some modification/revision of the earlier decision in *Ms. J v. ADB* [Decision No. 116], the Tribunal dismissed the same, on the ground that neither of them had satisfied the laid down conditions in Article XI of the Statute, which has to be strictly construed. The decision in *Ms. D's* case [Decision No. 111] is similar where the revision application was also not granted.

Apart from the aforesaid cases, in the majority of the other cases decided recently by the Tribunal and reported, it will be relevant to mention that some reliefs, like compensation for intangible injury, damages, or equitable compensation plus cost, have been given to the Applicants, while dismissing some of the other claims.

It will also be relevant to mention that in two decisions, namely Decision No. 114 and Decision No. 115 (para. 84 and para. 90), the Applicants had contested the bank's decision to terminate their employment under the 2016 Early Separation Program by the order dated 28 August 2017 and 29 September 2017, respectively. Both the Applicants had, *inter alia*, prayed for rescission of the aforesaid orders and compensation, which was granted by the Tribunal. However, as already pointed out (para. 90 *supra*) the Tribunal awarded a lesser amount of compensation and costs to the Applicant in Decision No. 114, taking into account his actions in filing a civil suit in another country against the bank officials, which was contrary to his terms and conditions of employment with the bank and constituted a "serious misconduct."

Therefore, in many cases, wherever appropriate, the Tribunal has awarded adequate remedy or relief to the Applicants (e.g., in the form of preliminary reliefs and compensation, including compensation for intangible injury, *ex-gratia* payment, equitable compensation, legal fees, and costs).

CONCLUSION

Therefore, with regard to the remedies/reliefs available to an Applicant, a member of the staff of the bank, the following are the concluding observations:

(i)   Any member of the bank staff, whether current or former member, can make an application to the Tribunal for adjudication in any case where the member alleges nonobservance of the contract of employment or terms of appointment as provided in Article 11, paras. (1) and (2) of the Statute, 1991.

(ii)   Normally, the Applicant has to exhaust all other remedies available within the bank, before filing the application to the Tribunal, except as decided by the Tribunal, where the Applicant and the President of the bank have agreed to the submission of the application directly to the Tribunal (Article II para. (3)).

(iii)   The aforesaid application to the Tribunal must conform to all the relevant provisions of the Statute and the Rules of Procedure 1992, before it can be admitted for adjudication by the Tribunal.

(iv)   The Applicant can seek all the remedies from the Tribunal, including preliminary measures, like oral hearing, anonymity, hearing *en banc* by the Tribunal, specific performance, rescission of the impugned decision, compensation and legal costs, as provided in the Statute and the Rules of Procedure.

(v)   Reasonable compensation to be paid to the bank, under Article X, para. 6, has not been granted by the Tribunal so far.

(vi)   In exceptional circumstances, the Tribunal can ask the bank to consider payment of an *ex-gratia* amount to the Applicant.

(vii)   The decisions of the Tribunal are final and binding (Article IX).

(viii) The Tribunal has exclusive jurisdiction to settle matters involving a staff member of the bank, on any matters relating to the service conditions, including conditions of terms of appointment, employment, and retirement.

(ix)   A staff member of the bank cannot seek any remedy, whether by way of a civil suit or a criminal complaint, in any other legal system of the member countries, who had signed the Agreement establishing the Asian Development Bank; the Tribunal has deprecated such action, especially when the Applicant has an application pending before the Tribunal.

(x)   The Tribunal can grant some compensation for intangible injury to the Applicant where the Respondent fails to follow its own procedures.

(xi)   An Applicant who filed an earlier case in which a judgment was delivered may file an application for clarification of that judgment of the Tribunal.

(xii)   An Applicant can file an application for review of an earlier decision of the Tribunal, subject to the conditions stated in Article XI of the Statute, which will be construed strictly.

An Independent, Just, and Accessible Tribunal Is Key to a Lasting Industrial Peace

Cesar L. Villanueva, Executive Secretary
Filemon Ray Javier, Legal Assistant to the Administrative Tribunal

I t is with honor and pride that the Office of the Executive Secretary (OES) joins the Asian Development Bank (ADB) community in celebrating the 30th Anniversary of the ADB Administrative Tribunal. Indeed, it is a milestone that commands celebration because it represents 30 years of providing independent and impartial determination of disputes relating to ADB staff contracts of employment and terms of appointment. Among other developments, it is truly worthwhile to consider that the very first executive secretary to serve upon the constitution of the Tribunal now sits as one of the judges of the Tribunal, Judge Raul Pangalangan, who concluded in May of this year his tenure with the International Criminal Court.

Considering that the OES is duty bound to "receive applications instituting proceedings and related documentation for each case submitted to the Tribunal," "maintain for each case a record of all documents received and sent, and of all actions taken, in connection with the case," and "attend hearings and meetings of the Tribunal," among other responsibilities, it can be said that it is at the forefront of ADB's efforts to ensure that its staff have an effective recourse regarding specific employment-related disputes with the bank.

All 125 judgments of the Tribunal have been rendered only after considered examination of, and deliberation on, the facts and rules involved in each case. More importantly, these decisions have been arrived at with utmost impartiality on the part of the judges, then and now. Since 1991 up to the present, OES has been acting as a bridge between the parties and the Tribunal. OES thus takes pride of its important role in ensuring that access to the Tribunal is always available in a prompt and efficient manner.

To be sure, the decisions of the Tribunal have created precedent to ensuring industrial peace within the bank over the last 30 years. At the risk of stating a hasty conclusion, one could surmise that whether the decision grants some form of relief to the Applicant (which comprises 35% of the promulgated decisions of the Tribunal) or dismisses the application altogether (which comprises 56% of the promulgated decisions of the Tribunal), the Tribunal necessarily provides a valuable lesson, and further clarifies the relationship between the staff and the bank for a healthier interaction moving forward.

We offer a random sampling of the Tribunal's notable pronouncements out of the many in the last 3 decades, which had or could have everlasting effects on how affairs are carried out in ADB:

- The Tribunal does not sit to review the determinations or recommendations of the Appeals Committee. Rather, it has jurisdiction to hear claims that decisions of officials acting on behalf of the bank have violated a staff member's contract of employment or terms of appointment. — *Alcartado v. ADB (No. 2), Decision No. 46, 19 December 1999.*

- The power to amend even a nonessential condition of employment, although within the discretion of the bank, is subject to the substantive and procedural restrictions properly imposed on all such discretionary decisions. It is the duty of the Tribunal to ensure that this discretionary power is not abused, and that the exercise by the bank of its discretion is not "arbitrary, discriminatory, unreasonable, improperly motivated, and has not been carried out in violation of fair and reasonable procedure." — *Lindsey v. ADB, Decision No. 1, 18 December 1992.*

- It is a well-established legal principle that the power to make rules implies in principle the right to amend them unilaterally. However, it is equally well established that there are limits to this power and that any changes must be reasonable and must respect the essential and acquired rights of staff. — *Perrin et al. v. ADB [No. 3], Decision No. 113, 21 July 2018.*

- There is no support for the view that an employer is absolutely liable to a staff member for injury suffered by him while on the employer's premises or otherwise performing the duties of an employee. The position is, rather, that, as a matter of the general principles of the law of employment, the bank owes to all members of its staff a contractual duty to exercise reasonable care to ensure their safety while on the bank's premises. — *Bares et al. v. ADB, Decision No. 35, 31 March 1995.*

- Staff members have a right of access to documents that relate to their personal or individual files. However, staff members have no right to receive "working papers" that are defined as preparatory materials generated for the exercise of managerial responsibilities, or those that deal with general staff matters. There is no right of access when the documents do not relate to an "individual staff action." — *Mr. F v. ADB, Decision No. 104, 6 August 2014.*

- Any enquiry into the performance or conduct of a staff member must be carried out in accordance with the requirements of due process of law, in such a way that the establishment of the truth or falsehood of allegations is not itself a subject of discretion but is the consequence of an objectively verifiable and rationally explicable examination of the facts. Where the continuance or not of a staff member's livelihood is involved, it is not sufficient to rely on unexplained or unsubstantiated beliefs or vague recollections. — *Lindsey v. ADB, Decision No. 1, 18 December 1992.*

- The principle of nondiscrimination requires that staff members in "the same position in fact and in law" be treated equally. — *Murray v. ADB, para. 47, Decision No. 91, 23 January 2009.*

- The filing of a criminal complaint against ADB and/or members of ADB management team or staff in the national legal system is a grave issue for an international institution, particularly as the staff member's grievance had not yet been resolved within the internal justice system. This act is a violation of a staff member's duties and responsibilities to ADB. — *Mr. H v. ADB, Decision No. 108, 6 January 2017.*

- It is scarcely open to disputation that an ADB official's act of receiving money from a supplier of ADB, in connection with an ADB transaction, would constitute serious misconduct. The amount of the money received may be comparatively modest, but receipt thereof may nevertheless constitute misconduct or unsatisfactory conduct. — *Gnanathurai v. ADB, Decision No. 79, 17 August 2007.*

- The evaluation of the performance of employees is a matter of managerial discretion. The Tribunal may not substitute its discretion in such matters for that of the bank. In any event, bank discretion is not unlimited, and the Tribunal must ensure that the exercise by the bank of its discretion is not arbitrary or adopted without due process. — *R. Keith Leonard v. ADB, Decision No. 92, 19 August 2009.*

The Tribunal understands that its decisions is a source of light that guides parties in navigating the area of uncertainty during controversies. Thus, as part of its desire to be more accessible, not only did the Tribunal make available the full text of its decisions, but it also undertook an indexing project, which is now available on the ADB webpage, that provides the readers snippets of its rulings.

In recent years, the Tribunal has focused its attention on keeping it accessible to individuals who wish to invoke its jurisdiction. In fact, the Rules of Procedure have been amended to allow electronic filing of applications and other pleadings with the Tribunal.

As the Tribunal marks its 30th Anniversary, one thing remains certain, that the Tribunal, with the assistance of OES, shall continue to be an independent, just, and accessible tribunal as a necessary part of the efforts of the bank and its staff to maintain industrial peace.

Again, we congratulate ADB, its staff, and the Tribunal as we all celebrate this momentous event.

Conversation with the Members of the ADB Administrative Tribunal—Transcript of the 6 August 2019 Townhall Meet

Conversation with the Members of the Administrative Tribunal is a townhall event held on 6 August 2019 at the ADB headquarters, Manila, Philippines. It was facilitated by Gillian Triggs (President), Shin-ichi Ago (Vice-President), Anne Trebilcock (Member), Chris de Cooker (Member), Raul Pangalangan (Member), Cesar Villanueva (Executive Secretary), and Christine Griffiths (Senior Attorney to the Administrative Tribunal). The event was a first in the history of the Tribunal where the Members and Secretariat met with staff, briefly explained the mandate of the Tribunal, its Statute and Rules of Procedure, and answered questions from the audience.

The Members and Secretariat of the ADB Administrative Tribunal were all present during their townhall event in ADB headquarters (photo by M. J. Rubio).

C. VILLANUEVA: Good morning ladies and gentlemen! Welcome to the conversation proceedings this morning before the members of the Administrative Tribunal who are all present. I am Cesar Villanueva, the Executive Secretary of the Tribunal. I have been in this post since 2011. Joining us also is Christine Griffiths. She has been in the Tribunal longer than I have been—since 2003. I think she was a teenager when she joined the Tribunal. Before we proceed, I would like to request everybody present to basically turn off their cellphones or put them into silent mode. Thank you.

On behalf of the Tribunal, we would like to thank everybody who is present, both physically or online, for joining us this morning. This is the first dialogue that the Tribunal, in its almost 30-year history, has undertaken. And we would like to acknowledge the presence online of field offices from the People's Republic of China (PRC) and Myanmar. Thank you for being with us. More than anything, special thanks has to be given to people who have made it possible for us to hold this morning's dialogue. We have the new Assistant Secretary Sona Shrestha, General Counsel Chris Stephens, and the Chair of the Staff Council, Au Shion Yee. Thank you so much for your support.

To lead us this morning in the conversation will be the President of the Administrative Tribunal. May I invite all of you to give a warm welcome to the former President of the Australian Human Rights Commission, Madam President Gillian Doreen Triggs.

G. TRIGGS: Thank you Cesar. Can I just reassure that we are so pleased to see you? This is the first time that we have this opportunity to talk to you about the Tribunal. And we are coming up to our 30th anniversary in 2021. And so, it is a perfect opportunity to think about why we are here, who we are, what it is that we purport to do, and to get some of your thoughts about the Tribunal and the way it works for the future. We do appreciate that many of you will be economists. You like to look at economic rationalism. You like some figures on a PowerPoint. We want to demystify if we can what this Tribunal is all about. We use, of course, legal language and some obscure phrases. If you read the Statute of the Tribunal, you might wonder what is it all about? How this works? I think if I would sum up why we are here, it is really because we want to show that we are independent, we have an objective view, and we hope to ensure that the staff of the Asian Development Bank have an understanding of our processes, to have trust in what we do and credibility for the judgments that we produce at the end of the day. So it is about transparency, about understanding why we are here, what we are trying to do, and achieving objective and independent judgment according to the rule of law as set out in our Tribunal. So, demystification is very much a part of what we are doing in understanding the Statute but also understanding our code of ethics which underpins the role of the independent Tribunal.

Before I go on, I would like to go through, if I may, the Statute very briefly and open it up for questions and general discussion because that is the core and purpose of today. I would like each member of the Tribunal to introduce themselves. And you can see that we are international. We bring civil and common law approaches to understanding how the Tribunal works. And we are very proud I think to build on the work of the Asian Development Bank over many years, our predecessors. And to see how we have an evolving jurisprudence that is special to the bank but also consistent with the jurisprudence of other international organizations, particularly banking organizations. But perhaps we could start with (Shin-ichi) Ago-san who is the Vice-President of the Tribunal.

S. AGO: Hello, good morning everybody. My name is (Shin-ichi) Ago, Vice-President of the Tribunal. I have been working here (the Tribunal) for 5 or 6 years. I am the second oldest of the Tribunal after Gillian.

G. TRIGGS: I take that as a compliment.

S. AGO: Well, I am not talking about physical oldness but seniority. My basic career is academic. I am a scholar in public international law. I have been teaching law for some 35 or 40 years. But in between, some decades ago, I used to work with the International Labour Organization (ILO) as an international official myself. But at this moment, for 25 years, I have been back in the academia. I have been teaching law in Kyushu University in the western part of Japan for 20 years. Now, I am teaching in Ritsumeikan University in Kyoto. I am now back in ILO as a member of the Committee of Experts on the Application of Conventions and Recommendations, a very long name and one of the oldest institutions or arrangements among the international organizations, to follow up and supervise the application of standards. That is all.

G. TRIGGS: Thank you (Shin-ichi) Ago-san. Now, who should I ask? Anne Trebilcock.

A. TREBILCOCK: Good morning everyone. It is a pleasure to be here. My name is Anne Trebilcock. I have been a member of the Asian Development Bank Administrative Tribunal since 2015. I am also a member of the Appeals Tribunal of GAVI which is the Global Alliance on Vaccination and Immunization. I have also been a neutral chair of the step below, the equivalent of your Appeals Commission (or Appeals Committee) at the European Bank for Reconstruction and Development (EBRD) and also the International Federation of Red Cross and Red Cross Societies. Before serving as a neutral in international organizations, I was, for many years, a staff member of the ILO where I held a number of different legal positions and ended up as the legal adviser which is the Director for Legal Services of the ILO. I am happy to say that in my time at the ILO, I had a number of occasions to do some work in Asia. So, I am very pleased to be part of this institution. Thank you very much.

C. DE COOKER: Good morning. I am Chris de Cooker. Thank you for coming. Looking back now, I think it is now more than 45 years that I have been active in international administrative issues. That does not make me younger. I started as an academic for almost 10 years then I became an international civil servant in a lot of technical organizations in Europe. I had early retirement in 2011. My wife disagreed. She said I never retired. And maybe she is right. Since then, I have been advising a lot of international organizations on their internal dispute resolution systems. I have become a judge on a number of tribunals. Just to follow your example, I am here on this Tribunal. I have been, since a few weeks (back) together with Anne (Trebilcock) on the Appeals Tribunal of GAVI. I am the President of the North Atlantic Treaty Organization (NATO) Administrative Tribunal which has an enormous workforce, so we have a lot of work. Too much actually. But that is statistics. That is for later. I am also sitting on the EBRD Administrative Tribunal. There is a fifth one in the pipeline, but I think I should stop there if not I am going to be divorced, I think. What else am I doing? I am also an independent chair of some appeals bodies similar to what Anne (Trebilcock) did. I am, at the moment, in the ITAC organization which is a very technical organization and an enormous building site for the time being in the south of France. It is a fascinating international cooperation. I am also on the billboard of the Global Fund which is in the same building as GAVI in Geneva. So, this is what I am doing at the moment.

G. TRIGGS: Thank you Chris. That is wonderful. Now, Judge Raul from the Philippines.

R. PANGALANGAN: Thank you, thank you Gillian. My name is Raul Pangalangan. I am the newest member of the Tribunal. I attended my first meeting yesterday. But you know, I was involved in the work of the Tribunal in 1991 when it was first established. Fresh from my studies in the US, I was asked by the bank to assist the first President of the ADB Tribunal, a British QC, Professor Lauterpacht of Cambridge. I am now a judge at the International Criminal Court at The Hague in The Netherlands. We try cases like war crimes, crimes against humanity, and genocide. I am relieved that I will be dealing with milder issues here at the ADB Tribunal. I am the President of the Trial Division of the court. We have a Pre-Trial, Trial, and Appeals Division. Before that, here in the Philippines, I was a professor of law at the University of the Philippines, and I was dean of the law school for a while.

G. TRIGGS: Thank you very much. And for my part, I am an international lawyer, public international lawyer. I first came to know the Asian Development Bank when I directed a couple of projects, one in Mongolia and one in Viet Nam on the rule of law in commercial matters, talking about the World Trade Organization rules and so on. I think across the group, we have got quite a range of experience and a real commitment to the objectives of the Asian Development Bank and to the understanding of the rule of law. We are a collaborative group and I think we work very well together in trying to reach the right answers to the matters that come before us. But I thought perhaps we would start by looking at the Statute. Now you are all equally capable of reading the Statute as of course, it determines our jurisdiction. But I thought I would go through it very briefly just to set the ground rules and then we can move on to a wider discussion.

> ## *Why do we need an ADB Administrative Tribunal?*
>
> - International organizations are legally immune from jurisdiction of national courts… leaves a justice gap
>
> - International rule of law requires access to courts and judicial process
>
> - Administrative tribunals enable staff to have complaints determined by independent judicial body

The first question is why do we exist? What is the point of administrative tribunals? People really in a wider arena have no comprehension of why you would have a tribunal for a major international banking organization. And it lies in the fundamental principle of immunity from the jurisdiction. And that is, the organization itself is immune from the domestic law. So that leaves the staff of the organization in a legal vacuum. So, it is imperative that they have access to justice. That is a fundamental principle of all the legal systems that we operate, i.e., there is a justice gap and it is necessary that staff and all those connected with the bank for that matter have access to rule-of-law-based means of resolving any disputes. As a matter of domestic laws within the bank, staff may not go to domestic tribunals. So, the idea then is that staff will appeal ultimately from the domestic processes within the bank itself to an independent body that can make a final and non-reviewable determination as a matter of law. I think it is important to understand this system as a whole, however, because what happens within the bank's processes to resolve a complaint are in some ways most important. Because if you go through those processes right, you do not need to come to us at all. And so, they do work together, but the Tribunal is of course separate from the bank and is independent of it in making its determinations.

> ## *Jurisdiction of the Tribunal*
> Article II
>
> - Tribunal *"shall hear and pass judgment"* on any application by a staff member alleging nonobservance by Bank of contract of employment or terms of employment, including:
>   - Regulations and rules
>   - Staff retirement plan and benefit plans
>   - No mandate to second guess management decisions
>   - Tribunal will focus on questions of due process

The jurisdiction of the Tribunal is determined by the Statute. We cannot make up matters we can cover. We must act according to the Statute determined of course by the Board of Directors for the bank itself. But you can see in Article II of the

Statute that we hear and pass judgment—rather a pompous word but nonetheless, we make the final determination on the application by a staff member that essentially alleges nonobservance by the bank of their contract of employment or terms of employment. That can include quite a range of things. The regulations and rules include the Staff Retirement Plan and benefit plans. But critically, I do not think it is understood as well as it might be, as a Tribunal, we do not have a mandate to second guess managerial decisions. I imagine many of you in this room make those managerial decisions. We do not interfere with those proper decisions. But we will ask the question, have you exercised due process? Have you followed your own rules of the bank and proper rights of access to the law when you made those managerial decisions? So, we have to tread quite a fine line in not interfering with the proper decisions you have made but to ensure that you have made them within the parameters of the rule of law.

Who are Tribunal Members?

Article IV

- Tribunal has five members of "high moral character" and qualified for high judicial office or competent jurisconsults

- Appointed by Bank's Board of Directors
  - President: Gillian Triggs
  - Vice President: Shin-ichi Ago
  - Member: Anne Trebilcock
  - Member: Chris de Cooker
  - Member: Raul Pangalangan

ADB Administrative Tribunal

- Members:
  - Appointed for 3 years, extensions up to 9 years
  - Entirely independent and cannot receive instructions from anybody
  - Must recuse (excuse from case) if any actual or potential conflict of interest
- Decisions with reasons are by majority vote and are final and binding
- Dissenting views may be included
- Tribunal establishes rules of procedure, oral hearings, and determines its competence and jurisdiction

---

Well, who are we? You know broadly speaking who we are. We must be, according to the Statute, of high moral character. And I think we make that very high standard, but we also have a code of ethics that ensures that we act in a way that is independent and objective. We act as judges, separate and independent from the bank itself. That is something that controls our behavior and that is ultimately accountable through provisions of the Statute and through the Board. We are appointed for 3 years, but we can be reappointed for up to 7 [actually, 9 years in total]. This is my seventh year which is why I am the most senior in years. That is all. We are first among equals. We cannot receive instructions from anybody. We must recuse ourselves or take ourselves out of a case if there is any conflict. It may be on occasions, one of us perhaps has given some legal advice as a lawyer some time ago on a matter, and we would be required to recuse ourselves from that judgment. So, it is really to enforce rigorously the idea that we are independent. We can give dissenting views, but I have to say, certainly in my experience, we have always reached a consensus view. We have not published (during the term of Judge G. Triggs) dissenting views. But we do not discourage them if someone does really have a good argument. We have robust argument up in there in an enclosed office of ours, room of ours on the 9th floor. We do have robust arguments and discussions, but we almost always reach a consensus view.

Although we are controlled by our Statute, we do establish our Rules of Procedure. We can have oral hearings if we choose. We can determine our own competence. We will, in fact, be embarking on something of a reform process just to bring the Rules of Procedure up-to-date in light of electronic filing and so on. So, you might see some reforms coming along to make it easier for people to operate electronically rather than in this world of paper.

Evolving Jurisprudence of ADBAT

- Decisions published in the Reports and online

- Role of comparative international administrative law developed by other international tribunals: ILO, WB, IMF, UN, etc.

We publish reports. I am really very proud to see—just in the relatively short time I have been with the bank—the growing number of published jurisprudence of the bank. That has been emerging. We do, of course, look at the jurisprudence of other similar organizations—the ILO, the World Bank Administrative Body (Tribunal), the International Monetary Fund (IMF), and the United Nations itself. So, we try to ensure that the broad principles of law, of due process, and the application of the principles of the Statute are implemented in a way that is consistent with emerging international jurisprudence. It does not have to be exactly the same, but we do learn from each other to build that body of consistent law for the, of course, very significant growth in international organizations, each of which will have some form of immunity from the jurisdiction of domestic law.

Who has access to the Tribunal?

- Current or former staff member of the Bank with regular fixed term appointment of 2 years or more
- Any person entitled to payment under Staff Retirement Plan or benefit, etc.

Now, current and former staff members of the bank with a regular or fixed-term appointment of 2 years or more can have access to the Tribunal and any person entitled to payment under the Staff Retirement Plan or Benefit. In other words, those who are really affected by the ways in which the bank's rules are applied.

Procedural Requirements

- Exhaustion of remedies available: *i.e.*: applicant must use all processes for resolution and appeal provided by Bank for complaints
- Application to be filed within 90 days of event leading to the application, or notice that relief is denied or delayed by 30 days

---

There is a very typical rule, and that is before coming to the Tribunal, you must exhaust the remedies that are available in the bank itself. In other words, unless you agree with the bank to skip those processes, and it does happen, in the main, you must meet the proper processes that the bank establishes. And the whole idea of course is to resolve those questions at a much earlier stage before the matter ever comes before the Tribunal. And of course, statistically, most matters are resolved that way, and resolved quite amicably, appropriately, and professionally within the bank.

There are some rules about filing. The application must be filed within 90 days of the event that has led to the application in the first place. It is approximately a 3-month period for notice that relief is denied or delayed.

Powers of Tribunal: Article X

If application well founded:

- Rescind decision of Bank
- Require specific performance of Bank's obligation
- Fix compensation no greater than 3 years' basic salary, unless exceptional circumstances
- Order reasonable costs, *e.g.*: legal counsel
- Refer back case to Bank to correct procedure
- Compensate Bank if application manifestly without proper basis

---

We have certain powers. We have quite significant powers. We can rescind a decision of the bank. That is quite a strong power if we choose to exercise it. We can require specific performance for the bank's obligation. If it has not met that obligation, we can require to do so. And the findings of course of the Tribunal are binding on the bank. We can fix compensation if we feel that is justified in the circumstances. Although there is a cap on that of 3 years, the Tribunal still has a very wide power to decide that there are exceptional circumstances and go beyond that sum. We can order reasonable legal cost. Perhaps, we do see a number of matters now where people have gone to law firms for legal advice, but that of course can raise very significant legal costs, and people need to be reassured that provided they have a case to answer, they will get reasonable costs to ensure that they have access to justice. And that is the key point of access to justice in what will otherwise be a legal vacuum. We can also refer our case back to the bank to correct their procedures. But this is the other side of the coin. If the application is manifestly without basis, then there is a risk that the Tribunal will compensate the bank itself which will also have to put considerable resources into dealing with the matter. So, it is a risk for anyone who manifestly has failed to have a proper basis for their application.

Rules of the ADB AT

- Tribunal President directs the work of Tribunal and Secretariat
- Tribunal is supported by Executive Secretary and staff
- Plenary session once a year and special plenaries
- A party may request all members sit on a panel and Tribunal has the power to do that
- Confidentiality

The President directs the work of the Tribunal. But as I say, we are highly collegiate. We work with the secretariat through Cesar (Villanueva) and through Christine (Griffiths). We meet every year. We must meet every year. But we probably meet in practice every 2 years. We had a very busy time in the last couple of years, particularly the last year. You could see that in the publication, the thickest volume of work that we are doing or have been doing, an increasing amount of case work over the last year or two which has been very intellectually stimulating for us. We really enjoyed doing the work. We have got a "quiet time" at the moment, which is why it has been a great opportunity to establish this conversation.

Typically, we sit together or what is termed as en banc. We can sit as a group of three but we typically work together as five. And we also operate on the principle of confidentiality of the Applicant. The Tribunal and I know the bank itself is not in the business of naming and shaming people. It is not what this is all about. So, confidentiality is a very important part of the process. And important indeed to achieving a just outcome, perhaps earlier than the matter comes to us.

Procedure: Rules and Practice Directions

Application through Executive Secretariat including:

- Request for preliminary or provisional measures
- Legal obligations of Bank
- Compensation requested
- Concise statement with facts and legal grounds
- Annexes and six copies (currently)

There are various rules and procedures, and I will not go into them, but through the Executive Secretariat, preliminary or provisionary measures can be asked for and compensation requested and assistance to ensuring concise statement of facts. There are various rules about annexes and copies, I will not go to any of that. Hopefully, because with electronic filing we can reform and make it much easier for everybody.

Procedural Rules

Applicant submits the **Application** within **90 days** upon compliance with Article II Para. 3(b)* of the Statute

⬇

Respondent (ADB) submits the **Answer** within **60 days** upon receipt of the Application

⬇

Applicant submits the **Reply** within **45 days** upon receipt of the Answer

⬇

Respondent submits **Rejoinder** within **30 days** upon receipt of the Reply

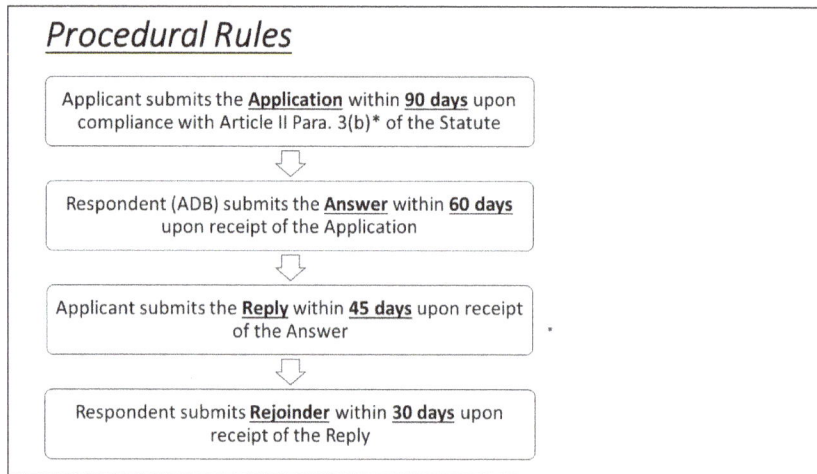

*Note: (i) the occurrence of the event giving rise to the application; (ii) receipt of notice, after the applicant has exhausted all other remedies available within the Bank, that the relief asked for or recommended will not be granted; or (iii) receipt of notice that the relief asked for or recommended will be granted, if such relief shall not have been granted within thirty days after receipt of such notice.

This is just a schematic approach on how this (application process) works, but it is quite an efficient system. And we are quite pleased with the relative speed with which the Tribunal can work. But we do understand that of course it can take a year or more for something to come through the bank itself. So, when you add this period of time on top of it, staff members can be a little aggrieved that they are not getting the outcome they want as quickly as they want. And I think perhaps we all work on that. But at the moment, an application within 90 days, the respondent submits an answer within 60 days. The Applicant then submits a reply within 45 days. Then the respondent (submits) with the rejoinder within 30 days. So, you can see a process of enabling the parties to out their case, to counter the arguments put by the other side so by the time the matter comes to the Tribunal, we have got a pretty complete statement of what arguments the parties want to make.

Procedural Rules

> Tribunal puts the case on the list. The Executive Secretary informs both Parties about the listing of the case.

⬇

> Tribunal holds a plenary session.

⬇

> The Executive Secretary issues Notice of Decision to both Parties.

⬇

> The Decision is published and archived on the Bank's website.

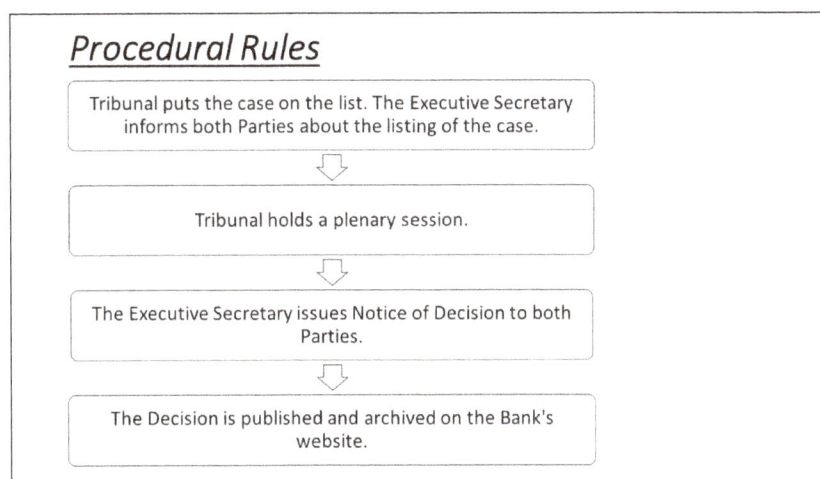

Then the Tribunal puts the case on the list for us to hear. The Executive Secretary really carries the matter to ensure the parties are aware of the listing. The Executive Secretary then will issue a notice of decision to the parties. It is then published and archived, and you can read all of our judgments if you want to understand why we reached a view on a matter that you may have strong feelings about. If you are surprised by the decision of the Tribunal, can I suggest that you really go back to the primary source and read the judgment. Why did we do it? There may be something that you are just puzzled about, and you just do not understand. You think you did the right thing, or your colleague did the right thing on a management decision and it has been seen as perhaps not quite the right thing by the Tribunal. Do take the time. One of the things we hope to do in the future is to produce summaries or head notes of the decisions, so they are easier to read. But it is worth taking the time to see why we reach a decision that might surprise you or might not totally meet your expectation.

Tribunal determination

- Oral proceedings under oath if Tribunal decides to admit
- Tribunal may call for additional evidence
- Affected persons may intervene and a person with a substantial interest in outcome may be a friend-of-the-court
- Tribunal or President may modify rules in exceptional cases

---

There are some technical points. We can receive oral proceedings under oath. We can call for additional evidence and we have done that. Affected persons can intervene. A person with a significant interest can be a friend of the court. And indeed, we can modify our rules in certain cases. So, there is a certain amount of flexibility in making a final determination. In other words, we may say we have gotten some of the story by the parties, but we have not gotten all of the story. And then we will go back and say we really do not understand how this is working. Why decisions were made the way they were? Can we have some more information? So that is quite an important part.

Revision of Judgment: Article XI

If, within 6 months of a judgment :

- A Party may request Tribunal to revise judgment
- Party discovers a fact *"which by its nature might have had a decisive influence"* on that judgment, and
- Fact unknown to both Party and Tribunal.

Now we give a judgment, but it is possible to, in a sense, ask for a revision of that judgment, which is quite an important part of any proper process. We are not always going to get it right every time, or much more importantly in reality, it is necessary to show that one of the parties has discovered a fact, a new fact which by its nature might have a decisive influence in the judgment. So, there is something missing that was not included in the judgment that would in fact have made a significant difference. And if that fact was unknown to both the party and the Tribunal, then the matter can be revisited. So, it is an important safeguard where something has been missed. But that really is the end of the story. And good law and good roles of the Tribunal is, there has to be an end to this process and that is non-reviewable.

So that is really a very quick run through. We have concentrated on the Statute rather than the rules and regulations because the Statute is determined by the Board. It is the Statute that determines our powers, and we must operate within those powers. But we are, as I say, coming up on our 30 years. It is time to look at some of the processes. Time to look at some possible gaps or ambiguities in the Statute. I think the Board and Chris (Stephens) and his staff had been thinking of looking at this rather at an early stage. So, we would be interested in any reforms that you have or any comments or any suggestions.

So now it is time then for an open discussion. We are very interested in your own thoughts and questions. So, I open it up to you. Thank you very much.

Staff had the opportunity to directly ask questions to the Members of the ADB Administrative Tribunal (photo by M. J. Rubio).

AUDIENCE 1: First of all, thank you very much for a very illuminating presentation. I think after 30 years, it is heartening to hear from the Administrative Tribunal. I got two questions actually. The first one actually is to each of the panel members. You mentioned on the Board there of course, there are reforms being thought about in terms of the Statute of the Administrative Tribunal. I would like to ask each member of the panel, what one change would you recommend, taking into account your own experiences and the fact that you sit on other panels of other international organizations? What changes you would think would be appropriate after 30 years in terms of the Statute? That is my first question to each of you. My second question is, to what extent does Manila play a role in the decision-making process? Because ADB is quite a little bit different from other international organizations. If an international organization has its headquarters in North America or in Europe, then one option is available to staff, and it is not a legal option but a practical remedy. It is to leave your organization and find another job. It could be to go to academia, certainly for international staff. Of course, national staff have different criteria. But for international staff, the practical remedy sometimes is, 'well okay, I will find another job somewhere else...go to academia, to commercial sector or work for another organization.' That option is actually not available for international staff in Manila. And having basically a huge commitment to come to Manila, and sometimes with family, to have that practical remedy is not just there. So, I just wondered, in terms of the Administrative Tribunal, whether that is a factor sometimes taken into account when looking into particular situations. Thank you.

G. TRIGGS: Thank you very much. Who would like to go first? We have been discussing possible reforms we have thought of. Perhaps, I will ask (Shin-ichi) Ago-san to go first.

S. AGO: Yes, actually, I do not think we should go rotate the answers among ourselves because we have decided this matter yesterday for the whole day. We have come, sort of to say, to a sort of conclusion that certain matters, after we revised and renewed, so that we, the Administrative Tribunal adapts itself to the current environment. And to that extent, perhaps each one may have slightly different priority in the proposal for amending the Statute and Rules. But I think we can talk in one voice in a way to answer to your first question. Shall I do it?

G. TRIGGS: Yes, because we developed thematic issues that (Shin-ichi) Ago-san can speak to.

S. AGO: From my memory, one of the things which our President already mentioned in the presentation is the very simple question of supplying six copies in the application which is almost inexplicable. That dates back 30 years ago when the electronic thing had not yet developed to such an extent like this time, like today. So, this is something that we should immediately change. And there are also questions about how to deal with—the second most important one which we discussed, the remedies, yes—the jurisdiction and remedies. Although it is not us to decide because the Statute of the Tribunal is decided by the Board of Directors and not by the Tribunal. The rules—we can decide by ourselves. So, it is up to the Board of Directors to decide (on) the jurisdiction. To what extent are we supposed to give remedies. What else? The access of those who are not enumerated in the Statute at this time, at this stage, like consultants and other persons who have less than 2-year contracts, whether they are available for the status to apply for the Tribunal. That is another basic question which we discussed and something that the bank has to address—I mean the Board of Directors to address in changing/modifying the Statute. Otherwise, when it comes to rules, the Tribunal can itself decide the changes for which we discussed a number of things. That is still ongoing. I may ask other colleagues to add.

G. TRIGGS: They are the basic things that we are looking at. But we have mentioned to the General Counsel and Staff representative (Staff Council) and we will see where they go. But that is as far as we can take at the moment. We are looking at a number of areas that I think would make the system clearer, fairer and open up its jurisdiction, and give us wider options as a Tribunal. So, I think it is an exciting time. But perhaps I can ask Anne to comment on the extent which we might look at the point you have just raised. That this might be seen as a slightly different organization. Establishing the Asian Development Bank here in Manila may raise other concerns for staff members that may not be true in Geneva or New York or Paris. The extent which we may look at that.

A. TREBILCOCK: I think just a general matter, the Tribunal will always look at what the Applicant has actually requested, the bank's position vis-à-vis what the request is and assess the situation based on the law and the facts. So, it is a bit difficult to speak to that question as a general matter.

G. TRIGGS: But we will certainly take it into account.

A. TREBILCOCK: It is clearly a reality. The Tribunal, of course, looks at the document before it, but it is also, you know, we are the people who are aware of what is going on in the world. So, I think to that extent that is just automatically taken into account. I would like to make one comment, if I may, in response to your original question. One element that will be quite important as the revision of the rules continues and that is to make sure that the drafting is as clear as possible. Thirty years ago, people were not very concerned about writing in what is called plain language or having clarity of legal provisions. I think contemporary tribunals understand that it is very important for the users of a tribunal to be able to readily understand how this system works, what are the rules I need to follow. So that will be in the back of our minds as we go forward.

G. TRIGGS: And the lady in the back. Did you have questions? Yes.

AUDIENCE 2: Thank you. It is very nice to see you. Thank you for this opportunity. I am not a lawyer so I am not sure if my question will be appropriate. But I am interested about the slide you showed me about the power of the Tribunal. If you can go back to that slide, please?

G. TRIGGS: Is this the one?

AUDIENCE 2: Yes. So, this is about the Tribunal talking to the bank and then the bank has to—so it is basically enforcement. So, you can enforce the bank to do and follow the judgment produced by the Tribunal. But how about the staff? How would you enforce or—I do not know how to say it. Is there any remedial action if the staff does not want to follow or respect the judgment? Because sometimes they win, sometimes they lose. Maybe the Tribunal decides to ask the staff to do something for the bank. Maybe they are sometimes misinterpreted. There are actions [that] the bank has made (or that they made the bank do so). So, I am interested in the other side of the coin. Thank you.

G. TRIGGS: Chris, would you like to have that one?

C. DE COOKER: I think it is very rare that the staff member has an obligation under a judgment. I do not know. You will write a decision that is annulled, and it is for the management to implement or correct that decision. If they do not, you can come back. Now the only situation that I can see is that where, and it is a very rare case and it has not happened yet luckily, is that the appeals is abusive and the bank made a lot of cost and we find it reasonable that you reimburse the bank. Now, if you do not do that, I think the bank has an action against you, and I think they have the means to convince you to pay. I do not think they will come to the Tribunal. Theoretically, it could be possible. I think that is my answer.

G. TRIGGS: I think there is a lady down the front. Maybe not. Then there is lady in the back. Thank you.

AUDIENCE 2: I am sorry but just an additional comment. Sometimes if the staff is gone or has gone somewhere, and you never know how to contact [them]. And it is difficult to make them pay any costs. I understand that the Tribunal decides for the staff but to be fair to the bank and staff. Sometimes I think, okay the bank has to be fair to the staff. But how can the staff be fair to the bank if there is any judgment from the Tribunal?

G. TRIGGS: As Chris said and in fact, I have not come across this example although he raised an important point. If the person is still within the bank's employment, it would not be difficult for the bank to insist on the compliance with the Tribunal's direction. If the employee has left the bank, at least 2 years later that this would start to be relevant. That staff member could be anywhere in the world and extremely difficult to deal with. I suspect that there is virtually nothing that can be done at that stage. And I do not think of the bank's vindictive processes. They want to have good relations with its former and past staff, and I think, mainly, things are resolved. In terms of absolute enforcement, it is extremely difficult in those cases. There is one case, for example, where a very, very important witness in a sense could not be contacted, and that made a big difference because it was impossible to make contact with that person. But there is nothing really that you can do about it. In terms of enforcement, in terms of the bank, well the bank will always abide by the rulings of the Tribunal. And indeed, the Board of Directors will make sure that would happen as representatives of the bank. But I take your point. It is a two-sided obligation. And staff members should accept the responsibility if they had been asked to do something by the Tribunal.

AUDIENCE 3: When a grievance [is] brought against a Vice-President, [it] would normally be processed within ADB's internal justice system by the staff reporting to that Vice-President, giving rise to their having actual or potential conflict of interest, and if in that process, those staff appear not to correctly interpret relevant administrative orders (AOs), will the Tribunal receive the grievance without it first being processed through ADB's internal justice system if those staff do not recuse themselves?

G. TRIGGS: So, you are saying, that because of a conflict of interest, it has become difficult for the matter to be dealt with in a fair way within the internal process?

AUDIENCE 3: If they do not recuse themselves.

G. TRIGGS: If they do not recuse themselves. I think we would look at an application, if an application set out those facts and they were objectively true, then I think we would probably talk to the bank to see skipping the internal process and bringing it to the Tribunal. And we have done that in one matter, not on those circumstances but on a different matter. There could be occasions where the bank and staff would say, 'we do not want to do the internal process, we will come (sic) straight to the bank.' And we will agree on that. If the circumstances arose that you are describing, I think you would certainly want to look at the internal process. But if you do not have faith in those internal processes because you are concerned about conflict of interest which I think is what you are saying, I think in the first instance, you would really want to work within that process to convince the senior staff within the bank that that conflict of interest should be eliminated.

In other words, take a simple case where somebody made a decision about a staff employee and that same person is sitting on the Appeals Committee in relation to the same matter. That is clearly a conflict of interest, and it would be managed within the bank itself. The counsel to the bank would advise that this is conflict and inappropriate. So, you would hope it would be resolved internally. In a very exceptional case where it was not resolved internally, then I imagine the Tribunal would at least look at it. But the preference would be that the matter should be resolved properly within the internal processes of the bank. But conflict of interest is an important point. It has come up in a number of matters that we have looked at. And it does need to be understood.

One of the suggestions we would like to make [would be that] perhaps we have a few training sessions with managers that make these decisions so that they understand what a conflict of interest is. And if people start to recognize that conflict, then they are much quicker or it is much easier for them to avoid that kind of hypothetical problem that you are describing.

C. DE COOKER: But the Tribunal also has the power to, as we explained, to send the matter back if we see that there was an issue that the pre-procedure was not correctly done, we can send it back and say 'do it correctly.' So, there is some guidance. But I hope that you are talking about hypothetical situation.

G. TRIGGS: Yes.

AUDIENCE 4: Thank you. Organizations have changed in 30 years, where earlier you would look at jobs for life; now organizations are mandated to be more nimble and agile, and go through various cycles of change. So, is the Tribunal looking at that? Are you looking at ways in which you can help the bank become more agile, maybe through rescaling of staff or maybe a more terminal solution? How are you kind of bringing that thinking into your reforms?

G. TRIGGS: Well, thank you and it is an important point. We are in a highly dynamic environment, and perhaps arguably and increasingly unstable one. We can only operate within the context of our Statute. But we would like, within the context of the Statute and Rules, that we determine to bring the processes up into a more contemporary environment. So, in that way, we hope that the bank could be more agile and efficient. An obvious one is the procedural matter, the e-filing. It could save paper, time, and frustration on all sides, and also could speed the process up which I would very much like to see. But that is an obvious answer. But there are other areas of substance, be it a contemporary improvement. There are changes in the international environment on this jurisprudence. One of them being the limits of immunity of international organizations that we are going to be looking at in the future. From your smile, I am sure you know what I am talking about. There are changes over time.

But certainly not our job to be advising the bank how to do or undertake their fundamental role. That is not for us at all. We are simply here as the absolutely last opportunity to resolve an issue of law for staff members. But we want [not only] to make that process as up-to-date as we can, but also to engage in contemporary ideas of what is discrimination, what is bullying in an office, when does a staff member not have the benefit of due process, and the problem of conflict of interest has come up. Quite innocently, I think perhaps there is a full understanding. But we hope if possible to have in the future training sessions and a bit more discussions like the one we are having now. Maybe even repeat this next year. Then we might be able to make the whole thing much more efficient which will be in the interest of the bank and its objectives (i.e., its much broader objective obviously in reducing poverty). We just had our photograph of the team in front of your information section and these are very inspirational pictures. We have to remind ourselves at the Tribunal, what it is that the Asian Development Bank does, why is it so inspirational, why is it so important. But we only play a very small role on that. But we want to make sure that the process works properly. Would you like to add something to that Judge Raul?

R. PANGALANGAN: Let me add something Gillian. I do acknowledge the point. [In] my own organization in the Netherlands, we are a court. The workflow depends upon the flow of the cases. And we do value—your term was a nimble organization and some flexibility. But the nature of a tribunal is to make decisions according to rules. So, in effect if you are saying that we should adapt to this need for flexibility and nimbleness, then it means that, theoretically, we have to be more, how should I say this, we lean over backwards, to be more lenient about decisions on termination. But that is not the function of a tribunal. We have rules to follow. And the legitimacy of a tribunal depends/flows from our adherence to those rules, the strict rules of jurisdiction—the application of rules impartially between the Applicant staff member and the bank. And I think the operational needs that you refer to are things that should be handled from your side of the fence. The way you write the terms of employment, the terms of engagement. But once those terms are written out, it is our solemn duty to just carry out those terms. We do not look beyond them.

G. TRIGGS: Is the lady in the white cardigan? And then the gentleman next to her.

AUDIENCE 5: Thank you for this conversation. Just one question. You mentioned that your body of work has increased significantly recently. I would like to know if you have reason for that. Do you know why is that? Is it because we are entering a period where people just have more legal, how can I say that—to push forward more? Or is it specific cases? Or is it because, perhaps, the Statute needs updating. If you have any insights.

G. TRIGGS: Well, thank you. Well, I should explain that because I did say that. I think it seems to go in spikes. You get a spike of work. And I am talking to Christine (Griffiths) and Cesar (Villanueva) about this for being involved in the bank for many years, and Judge Raul, of course, originally. The workload is increasing but it can decline to a very little for a year or two and then it will come up again. This year, we have got very little, in fact no work. And next year, we have got other cases in the pipeline. So, we have gotten a year where we have very little, hence this opportunity. The opportunity to think about broader questions of performance, of the Statute, and the rules and regulations. But last year we have, speaking generally, I do not want to speak particular cases, two matters that are extremely complex. And they were split into different elements. And they took a great deal of time. So, I think it is fair to say over the last couple of years, we have had some important substantive legal issues to determine whether they are very complex factual situations and that led to a significant increase in the workload. And we have now completed those matters. I do not think it reflects very much on what we can easily say; the fact that we have gotten nothing at the moment reflects the fact that the bank's internal process is now better, and we are not getting as many matters coming to us. I hope that is the case. But as I say, I am advised by those with the longer history in the bank that it always comes in spikes. It depends on what the issues are. I do firmly believe this is a continuous process. If the bank's internal processes are improved or better understood and implemented, then we should see fewer cases coming to the Tribunal. And that would really be the best outcome. Because you come into a world of strict law and rules. As Judge Raul said, we must apply the rule of law where if you are operating within the bank's processes, it is possible to look at things from a flexible angle to reach compromises, to reach sensible solutions. And that gives a better outcome very often for practical purposes.

AUDIENCE 6: Yes, thank you very much for this opportunity today. We really appreciate this. I have two questions for you. The first one is our administrative orders have a long history, but they are being updated regularly. How do they compare to other practices of organizations? I think our, you know, environment becomes more complex. What are the main gaps that you would see that would need to be...?

G. TRIGGS: I will stop you there before we make it to your second question because Anne (Trebilcock) has a lot of experience of looking at this. So, I will ask Anne to respond with a few words.

A. TREBILCOCK: I think I will respond by not responding because it is really not the role of the Tribunal to do an overview review of the rules of the institution to which they are connected. As Judge (Raul) Pangalangan has emphasized and President Triggs, we really are confined by and directed by the jurisdictional remit that we have been given. We will look at administrative order when it comes to us in the context of a case. And we will look at, not just necessarily how it has been applied, but perhaps, is that administrative order itself flawed in some ways that we will be able to point out. But we will not go then into a long discourse about how this is better conceived or less well conceived than comparable instruments in another organizations. We really think that is the role of management, to do that sort of research and examination. So, we will always look at administrative orders in the context of a particular question that is put to us.

G. TRIGGS: I think that is right. As I have said, perhaps briefly, we look at the comparative jurisprudence of other tribunals and we look at their statutes and see if they are different, which might explain difference in the outcome of a particular substantive matter. So, while we do that comparative exercise, I imagine you would want to do it and look at your administrative orders. Is this a sort of thing that other similar bodies would do? So, I think that process of comparative understanding of what is going on globally is a very healthy process. And it means we are all looking to make sure that we get the best possible procedures that ultimately, one way or another, deal with the rule of law. What is a fair and an appropriate way of dealing with this issue? It is a healthy thing to do. But it is not for us. I did want to make that point. We are not here to second guess management's decisions. That is not our job. That (if) you have met fundamental rules of law.

I think perhaps we can have one last question, if there is one.

AUDIENCE 6: The second (question) if I may.

G. TRIGGS: I am sorry. I beg your pardon.

AUDIENCE 6: The second question is really going back to the conflict-of-interest question. This is more of a question to you and your capacity and your experience rather, because we understand that there is a framework for you in this tribunal, but let us say from your experience as a judge, what in your views are solutions in other international organizations where the independence of management and decision-making is better established? And I am not saying it is bad here. I'm just saying it is a challenge. You know, on the one side, you are representing the respondent. On the other side, you are judging on the early stage of, let us say, a grievance process. So have you in your experience heard something about being a neutral member bringing in some outside views. So, the question is really what from your experience are practical ways to address conflict of interest?

G. TRIGGS: Can I just be clear? You are talking about the possible conflict of interest of a judge or management conflict of interest? Well, it is the same, it is the same answer really. Would you like to embark on that Chris (de Cooker)?

C. DE COOKER: I do not think, as you have said you have some views on that. But I would have to take off my hat as a judge and it is a little bit difficult sitting here as a judge. I find it difficult to answer such a question from this podium. If you like, we can chat maybe another day if it is understood that I am not a judge.

G. TRIGGS: But I do think that, in the value of this exercise, and one more question and we must really finish because you all have got to get back to your offices for sure and we want to keep it fairly precise. But it might be that we can follow this discussion along in the future through the bank. Because as I said, our job is dependent, in part, on how well you do your job within the organization. And if there are conflicts of interest or no clear understanding of what conflict of interest is, then that creates problems and that is how matters come to us. So, it will be much better to deal with the matter that concerns you in the bank and management, so we do not have to see the matter at the end of the day. So, it might be something the counsel or others within the bank would like to take up as a discussion. But that is the value of having this conversation frankly. And I hope we can keep doing this.

So, one last question, I think. Yes, I think the lady in the back.

AUDIENCE 7: So, I am not an economist, but I will ask questions about statistics. I hope that is okay. I was wondering, do you collect data on the types of cases that you get? For example, is it a case of compensation, about benefit, about discrimination, bullying? And do you keep statistics about how they are judged like in favor of the Applicant or in favor of ADB? Does it go back to ADB for reconsideration? And also, are the judgments disaggregated by, for instance, gender? How many women or men or age or level or nationality? Just to have some...

G. TRIGGS: The simple answer is we do not. But a better answer than we do not is we are aware of trends. But at the moment, Christine (Griffiths) as the Senior Attorney assisting the Secretariat is preparing an index of cases that (Shin-ichi) Ago-san held up. In other words, we have now a sufficient body of work for staff to draw some of those conclusions. It might be how many conflict-of-interest cases are there? How many employees are not satisfied with the payout? Or where they have been let go in circumstances that they do not think were fair, how many? We do not yet know. It is a sort of thing that could emerge from this indexing process. Then we can move on to the process of collecting some data. But I forget, Christine, how many cases have [we] had so far? One hundred twenty-two. Now that is really starting to build a body of law and jurisprudence. We do not have to rely as much on the comparative jurisprudence like when we did when I first arrived. It is much easier for us. So, it is a terrific question. We will keep that in mind. But I think it is going to start emerging as we start doing our own indexing and pulling together the jurisprudence over this nearly 30 years. So, it might be something that we can be producing in anticipation of celebrating our 30 years in 2021.

The Administrative Tribunal welcomed feedback and suggestions from staff particularly on the plan to establish reforms on the Statute and Rules of Procedure (photo by M. J. Rubio).

But I do think we need to finish now. I am sorry about the lady in the back. I think we are very happy to speak with you after this session. But I know many of you need to get back to your offices. But from my point of view and I am sure from the Tribunal members, it is a real pleasure to have a chance to talk to you directly. It is an honor to serve the bank as member of the Tribunal and help you achieve these remarkable objectives of the bank in achieving poverty reduction and development within this region. Thank you all for your work. I hope that we see you in a year or so and continue this discussion. Thank you very much.

Appendix 2
Introduction to the Revisions of the Rules of Procedure of the ADB Administrative Tribunal

The Tribunal has revised its Rules under the Statute of the Tribunal, taking into account developments in the field of dispute resolution in the international civil service, experience under the previous Rules, and changes in technology. Prior to adoption of the revisions, the Tribunal provided the Bank and the Staff Council with an opportunity to comment on the draft Rules. The Tribunal adopted the revised Rules through an electronic meeting of its Members on 10 February 2021. These Rules apply to applications submitted on or after 1 March 2021.

Certain revisions address powers of the President and the Executive Secretary (Rules 3 and 4); the notification, location, and means of holding Tribunal sessions (Rule 5(3) and (4)); submission of an application by electronic means or in paper copy (Rule 6(1)); some details to be supplied in accordance with amended Annexes I and II to the Rules; requests for anonymity (Rules 6(3) and Rule 7(3)); details regarding annexes to be furnished (Rule 6(6)); clarification of time limits for filing an application (Rule 6(9) and (10)); dismissal of a clearly inadmissible application (Rule 6(12) and (13)); aspects governing oral proceedings (Rule 11); and provisions on intervention, third parties, and amicus curiae (Rules 16 and 17).

Newly introduced rules concern recusal of a Member of the Tribunal (Rule 5(10) and (11)); preparation of an annual report of the Tribunal (Rule 3(3)); anonymous notification of a filing (Rule 6(15)); changes to the time frames for handling a preliminary objection to jurisdiction (Rule 7(1)), the Applicant's reply (Rule 8(1)), and the Bank's rejoinder (Rule 9(1)); timing of an application for costs (Rule 13); the possibility of an amicable settlement or withdrawal of an application (Rule 14); provisional measures in exceptional cases (Rule 18); consolidation (Rule 19); deliberations of the Tribunal (Rule 20); advance provision of a decision or judgment to the parties prior to its publication (Rule 21(2)); correction of a judgment in case of clerical or arithmetic error (Rule 22(1) and (3)); and addition of references to practice directions and the Tribunal's Code of Ethics (Rules 23(2) and 24).

Under the new rules, applicants and the Bank are no longer required to submit six copies of pleadings. Signatures may now be provided electronically. The revisions also make some minor changes to simplify or clarify wording (such as in Rule 15 on remand), and to employ "he or she" / "him or her" in the text. The Rules now feature a table of contents and additional headings. In a few cases, the order in which the rules appear has changed.

Revised Rules of Procedure of the ADB Administrative Tribunal

(Rules established under Article VI of the Statute. As revised on 10 February 2021)

Table of Contents

SECTION I: Organization

Rule 1

Term of Office of Members

Subject to any contrary decision of the Board of Directors of the Asian Development Bank (hereinafter referred to as the "Bank"), the term of office of members of the Tribunal shall commence on the first day of October of the year of their appointment by the Board of Directors of the Bank.

Rule 2

President and Vice-President

1.   The Tribunal shall elect a President and a Vice-President for terms of three years. The President and the Vice-President thus elected shall take up their duties immediately. They may be re-elected. Unless indicated otherwise, references in these rules to the "President" and "Vice-President" mean these individuals.

2.   Upon the expiration of the term of office of the President, the Vice-President shall act as President until a successor is elected. Upon the expiration of the term of office of the Vice-President, the senior member of the Tribunal shall act as Vice-President until a successor is elected.

3.   If the President or the Vice-President ceases to be a member of the Tribunal or ceases to hold office before the expiration of the normal term, the Tribunal shall elect a successor for the unexpired portion of the term.

4.   The election of the President or the Vice-President shall be by vote or assent of a majority of the members of the Tribunal, at a plenary session or by correspondence.

Rule 3

Duties of President and Vice-President

1.   The President shall direct the work of the Tribunal and of its Secretariat. The President shall represent the Tribunal in all administrative matters and shall preside at sessions and meetings of the Tribunal.

2.   The President may, as may be required, make orders for the conduct of proceedings and deal with any necessary matter not expressly provided in the present Rules, when permitted by the Statute.

3.   The President shall prepare an annual report on the activities of the Tribunal, which shall be published.

4.   If the President is unable to act, the Vice-President shall act as President.

Executive Secretary and Staff

1.   Under the authority of the President, the Executive Secretary of the Tribunal shall:

(a)   Receive applications instituting proceedings and related documentation for each case submitted to the Tribunal, including electronically;

(b)   Transmit all documents and make all notifications required, including electronically, in connection with proceedings before the Tribunal;

(c)   Maintain for each case a record of all documents received and sent, and of all actions taken, in connection with the case, including the dates thereof and of their receipt by or dispatch from the Executive Secretary's office;

(d)   Attend hearings and meetings of the Tribunal when instructed by the President;

(e)   Keep minutes of these hearings and meetings when instructed by the President;

(f)   Facilitate the transmittal of the transcript of notes or recordings in case of oral proceedings before the Tribunal;

(g)   Arrange for the public notifications required under these rules and for publication of the judgments and final decisions of the Tribunal;

(h)   Maintain the archives of the Tribunal;

(i)   Assist the Tribunal in issuing practice directions relating to pleadings and hearings;

(j)   Expeditiously carry out the above tasks and others assigned by the President.

2.   In addition to the Executive Secretary, the Tribunal shall have such other staff as it may deem necessary, who shall be placed at its disposal by the President of the Bank. The Executive Secretary, if unable to act, shall be replaced for the time being by a person appointed by the President of the Bank in consultation with the President of the Tribunal.

SECTION II: Sessions, Panels, and Recusal

Rule 5

Plenary Sessions

1.   The Tribunal shall hold a plenary session once a year on a date fixed by the President for the purpose of hearing cases, forming panels, and any other matters

affecting the administration or operation of the Tribunal including, if necessary, the election of the President and the Vice-President. When, however, there are no cases on the list referred to in Rule 13, paragraph 1, and no other business which in the opinion of the President would justify the holding of a session for their consideration, the President may, after consulting the other members of the Tribunal, decide to hold the plenary session on a later date.

Special Plenary Session

2.   A special plenary session may be convened by the President when, in his or her opinion, the number or urgency of cases requires such a session or it is necessary to deal with a question affecting the operation of the Tribunal.

Notice of Session

3.   Notice of the convening of a plenary session or a special plenary session shall be given to the members of the Tribunal at least thirty (30) days in advance of the date of the opening of such a session. The dates of the session shall be publicly notified in advance.

Location and means of holding sessions

4.   The Tribunal shall ordinarily hold its sessions in person at the Bank's headquarters. The Tribunal may decide to hold a session at another location or by electronic means, taking into account the prevailing circumstances, and the need for fairness and efficiency in the conduct of proceedings.

Quorum

5.   Three members of the Tribunal shall constitute a quorum for plenary sessions.

Panels

6.   In accordance with Article V of the Statute, the President, in consultation with the Vice-President, shall determine whether a case warrants consideration by a panel consisting of all its members or by a panel of three members, and the composition of any panel of three members.

7.   A party may make a written request, giving reasons, that the case be heard by all the members of the Tribunal. Such request shall be made, at the latest, by the Applicant in the reply filed under Rule 8, and by the Bank in the rejoinder filed under Rule 9.

8.   The President shall be the presiding member of any panel of which he or she is a member. If the President is not a member of a panel, the Vice-President shall be the presiding member of the panel if he or she is a member of it. If neither the President nor the Vice-President is a member of a panel, the President shall appoint one member to be the presiding member of that panel.

9.   The presiding member of a panel shall exercise all the functions of the President of the Tribunal in relation to cases before that panel.

Recusal

10.   In accordance with Article V, paragraph 5 of the Statute, a member of the Tribunal shall recuse himself or herself from a case if there is an actual or potential conflict of interest, such as:

(a)   having a personal, familial or professional relationship with a person involved in the case;

(b)   having been called upon previously in another capacity, such as advisor, representative, expert, or witness, in relation to the matter;

(c)   there being any other circumstances that would make participation in the case inappropriate.

11.   When assigned to a case, a member recusing himself or herself shall immediately inform the President of the Tribunal, who shall take action as needed. When the President recuses himself or herself, the Vice-President shall act as the President in that case.

SECTION III: Proceedings

Rule 6

Content of Application

1.   An application instituting proceedings under Article II of the Statute shall be submitted electronically to the Tribunal, addressed to ***admintribunal@adb.org***, or in paper copy addressed to the Office of the Administrative Tribunal at the Headquarters of the Bank.

An application shall be divided into four sections, which shall be entitled, respectively:

I.   Information regarding the personal and official status of the Applicant;

II.   Pleas;

III.   Explanatory Statements; and

IV.   Annexes.

2.   The information concerning the personal and official status of the Applicant shall be presented in the form contained in Annex I of these rules or its electronic equivalent.

Request for Anonymity

3.   At the time of instituting proceedings or at the latest upon filing a reply, the Applicant may request that his or her name, or the name of any witness or person cited, remain anonymous. The Applicant shall provide reasons for the Tribunal in support of such a request.

Pleas

4.   The section on pleas shall indicate all the measures and decisions which the Applicant is requesting the Tribunal to order or take. The pleas shall specify

   (a)   any preliminary or provisional measures, such as the production of additional documents or the hearing of witnesses, which the Applicant is requesting the Tribunal to order before proceeding to consider the merits;

   (b)   the decisions which the Applicant is contesting and whose rescission is requested under Article X, paragraph 1 of the Statute;

   (c)   the obligations which the Applicant is invoking and the specific performance of which is requested under Article X, paragraph 1 of the Statute;

   (d)   the amount of compensation claimed by the Applicant in the event of use of the option given under Article X, paragraph 1 of the Statute; and

   (e)   any other relief, including an application for costs, which the Applicant may request in accordance with the Statute.

Explanatory Statement

5.   The explanatory statement section shall set out concisely the facts and the legal grounds on which the pleas are based. It shall specify, *inter alia*, the provisions of the contract the nonobservance of which is alleged.

Annexes

6.   The annexes section shall contain the texts of all documents referred to in the application in accordance with the following rules:

   (a)   the Applicant shall certify that each document submitted is a true copy;

   (b)   documents that are not in English shall be accompanied by any necessary translations, certified by the translator;

   (c)   where only part of a document is relevant to the application, only such part, including the citation, shall be annexed; and

   (d)   every endeavor shall be made to avoid annexing or otherwise presenting a document more than once.

Presentation of Case; Representation of the Applicant

7.   An Applicant may present his or her case before the Tribunal, in written form or, if allowed pursuant to Rule 11, paragraph 1, in oral proceedings. The Applicant may designate any person to represent him or her before the Tribunal.

Authentication

8.   The Applicant shall sign the last page of the application. The Applicant may instead, by means of a letter transmitted for that purpose to the Executive Secretary, authorize signature by his or her designated representative. In the event of the Applicant's incapacity, the required signature shall be furnished by his or her duly authorized representative. Signatures may be provided electronically.

Time Limits for Filing an Application

9.   The Applicant shall file the application with the Executive Secretary within ninety (90) days after the latest of the following, taking into account Article II, paragraph 3(b) of the Statute:

   (a)   the occurrence of the event giving rise to the application;

   (b)   receipt of notice, after the Applicant has exhausted all other remedies within the Bank, that the relief asked for or recommended will not be granted;

   (c)   receipt of notice that the relief asked for or recommended will be granted, if such relief shall not have been granted within thirty (30) days after receipt of such notice; or

   (d)   the date of communication of the contested decision of the Pension Committee of the Bank to the party concerned.

If the President of the Bank and the Applicant have agreed to submit the application directly to the Tribunal in accordance with the option given to them under Article II, paragraph 3(a) of the Statute, the filing shall take place within ninety (90) days of the date on which the President of the Bank notifies the Applicant of agreement for direct submission.

10.   The date of filing shall be considered as the first of these dates:

   • the date on which the Applicant submitted a complete application electronically, or
   • the date on which the Executive Secretary received one complete paper copy of the application.

Corrections to the Application

11.   If the filing requirements of this rule are not fulfilled, the Executive Secretary may call upon the Applicant to make the necessary corrections to the

application within a period which the Executive Secretary shall prescribe. With the approval of the President, the Executive Secretary may make the necessary corrections when the defects in the application do not affect the substance.

Dismissal of Clearly Inadmissible Application

12.   If the President considers that an application is clearly inadmissible, he or she may instruct the Executive Secretary to take no further action pending implementation of paragraph 13 of this Rule. This instruction shall suspend all procedural time limits.

13.   In the circumstances mentioned above, the President shall, following consultation with the other members of the Tribunal, either dismiss the application as clearly inadmissible or order that the application shall proceed in the ordinary way.

Transmission to the Bank for Response; Bank Representation

14.   After ascertaining that the filing requirements for an application have been met, the Executive Secretary shall provide a copy of the application to the Bank for its response. The Bank may designate any person to represent it before the Tribunal.

Public Announcement of Filing

15.   Shortly after notifying the Bank of the application, the Executive Secretary shall publicly announce the date of its filing, its number, and a summary of the relief sought, without disclosing the identity of the Applicant or any other person.

Rule 7

Preliminary Objection to Jurisdiction

1.   If the Bank objects to the exercise of jurisdiction by the Tribunal, and seeks a decision on this point before filing the answer, the Bank may file a written objection within fifteen (15) days of provision of the application to it. Upon the filing of such objection, the President may suspend proceedings on the merits. The Applicant shall present written observations on the objection within fifteen (15) days of receipt thereof. If the President considers it necessary, additional pleadings on the objection may be required. After considering the pleadings, the Tribunal or, when not in session, the President shall either uphold the objection, reject it, or declare that it shall be joined to the merits of the case. As appropriate, the President may then fix a new date for the Bank to file its answer.

Filing of the Answer

2.   Within sixty (60) days of the date on which the application is provided to the Bank by the Executive Secretary, the Bank shall submit its answer to the Tribunal electronically or in paper copy. The answer shall include pleas, an explanatory statement, and annexes. The annexes shall contain all documents

referred to in the answer that are not already annexed to the application. They shall be presented in accordance with the rules established for the application.

3.   When filing its answer or, if required, its rejoinder, the Bank may request that the name of any witness or person cited remain anonymous. The Bank shall provide reasons for such a request.

Authentication

4.   The Bank's representative shall sign the last page of the answer. Signature may be provided electronically.

Transmission of Answer to the Applicant

5.   After ascertaining that the filing requirements have been complied with, the Executive Secretary shall provide a copy of the answer to the Applicant.

Rule 8

The Reply of the Applicant

1.   The Applicant may, within thirty (30) days of the date on which the answer is provided to him or her, file with the Executive Secretary a written reply to the answer, electronically or in paper copy. If the President decides it necessary, he or she may direct the Applicant to file a reply. The reply must be concise and avoid repetition of assertions made in the application as well as any new pleas.

2.   Any document referred to in the reply which had not been previously submitted to the Tribunal shall be annexed to the reply in accordance with the rules established for the application.

3.   The reply shall be signed in accordance with the rules established for the application. Signature may be provided electronically.

4.   After ascertaining that the filing requirements of this rule have been complied with, the Executive Secretary shall provide a copy of the reply to the Bank.

Rule 9

The Rejoinder of the Bank

1.   The Bank may, within twenty (20) days of the date on which the reply was provided to it, file a written rejoinder to the reply, electronically or in paper copy. The President may direct the Bank to file a rejoinder if he or she decides that it is necessary. The rejoinder must be concise and avoid repetition of statements in the answer.

2.   Any document referred to in the rejoinder which had not been previously submitted to the Tribunal shall be annexed to the rejoinder in accordance with the rules established for the application.

3.   The Bank's representative shall sign the last page of the rejoinder. Signature may be provided electronically.

4.   After ascertaining that the filing requirements have been complied with, the Executive Secretary shall provide a copy of the rejoinder to the Applicant.

5.   Unless Rule 10 is applied, the written proceedings shall be closed after the rejoinder, if one has been filed or, if not, after the reply has been filed.

Rule 10

Additional Statements, Documents, and Information

1.   In exceptional cases, the President may, on his or her own initiative, or at the request of either party, call upon the parties to submit additional written statements or additional documents within a period which he or she shall fix. The additional documents shall be furnished in the same manner as other submissions. When necessary, a document shall be accompanied by a translation into English.

2.   Each written statement and additional documents shall, on receipt, be communicated by the Executive Secretary to the other party, unless at the request of the submitting party, the Tribunal decides otherwise. The personnel files communicated to the Tribunal shall be made available to the Applicant by the Executive Secretary in accordance with the instructions issued by the Tribunal.

Obtaining Information

3.   In order to complete the documentation of the case prior to its being placed on the list for decision by the Tribunal, the President may obtain any necessary information from any party, witnesses or experts. The President may designate a member of the Tribunal or any other disinterested person to take oral statements. Any such statement shall be made under oath or declaration and provided to the parties in accordance with paragraph 2 above.

Production of Documents and Inquiry

4.   The Tribunal may at any stage of the proceedings call for the production of documents or of such other evidence as may be required. It may arrange for any measures of inquiry as may be necessary.

Rule 11

Oral Proceedings

1.   Oral proceedings, including the presentation and examination of witnesses or experts, may be held only if the Tribunal so decides, on its own motion or at the request of a party filed up to the date fixed for filing the rejoinder.

2.   By a date set by the President of the Tribunal sufficiently in advance of any oral proceedings, each party shall inform the Executive Secretary and, through him or her, the other party, of the names and description of proposed witnesses and experts. For each application for hearing a witness or expert, the party shall indicate the points to which the evidence is to refer. The Tribunal shall decide on each application and determine the sequencing of any oral proceedings.

3.   The Tribunal may decide that witnesses or experts shall reply in writing to any written questions posed. The parties shall, however, retain the right to comment on any such written replies.

4.   Practice directions of the Tribunal may provide further instructions on the conduct of oral proceedings.

Rule 12

Oral Evidence

1.   The Tribunal may examine witnesses and experts. The parties or their representatives or lawyers may, under the control of the President, put questions to the witnesses and experts.

Oath or Declaration

2.   Each witness shall make the following oath or declaration before giving evidence:

> *"I solemnly swear/declare upon my honor and conscience that I will speak the truth, the whole truth and nothing but the truth."*

Each expert shall make the following oath or declaration before making a statement:

> *"I solemnly swear/declare upon my honor and conscience that my statement will be in accordance with my sincere belief."*

Exclusion of Evidence

3.   The Tribunal may exclude evidence which it considers irrelevant, frivolous, or lacking in probative value. The Tribunal may also limit the oral testimony if it considers the written documentation adequate.

Rule 13

Listing of the Case for Decision

1.   When the President considers the documentation of a case to be complete, he or she shall instruct the Executive Secretary to place the case on the list for decision, and the Executive Secretary shall inform the parties as soon as the case is listed. Other than an application seeking reasonable costs as foreseen in Article X, paragraph 2 of the Statute, no additional statements or documents may be filed after the case has been included in the list, unless the Tribunal otherwise permits or requires.

Application for Costs

2.   An application for costs as permitted under Article X, paragraph 2 of the Statute may be submitted within ten (10) days of receipt of notification of the listing of a case.

Rule 14

Application for Adjournment

1.   Any application for the adjournment of a case shall be decided by the President or, when the Tribunal is in session, by the Tribunal.

Withdrawal of Application

2.   Should the Applicant notify the Tribunal that he or she is withdrawing the application, the President may accept the withdrawal without convening the Tribunal, as long as the withdrawal is unconditional. The withdrawal shall be noted in the archives of the Tribunal.

Amicable Settlement

3.   The Tribunal or, when it is not in session, the President may encourage mediation or direct discussions aimed at facilitating an amicable settlement of the application. With the consent of the parties, the proceedings will then be suspended. If a settlement is not reached, the proceedings will resume.

4.   If a settlement is reached, the President may accept it without convening the Tribunal, and proceedings will end. The result shall be noted in the archives of the Tribunal.

5.   No opinion expressed, suggestion, proposal, concession, or other document drawn up for the purpose of seeking an amicable settlement may be relied on for any purpose by the Tribunal or by the parties to the proceedings.

SECTION IV: Remand of a Case

Rule 15

Remand

1.   If, prior to a determination on the merits, the Tribunal finds that a procedure prescribed in the rules of the Bank has not been observed, the Tribunal may notify the parties accordingly in order to permit a request for institution or correction of the required procedure, in application of Article X, paragraph 3 of the Statute.

2.   If a request permitted under Article X, paragraph 3 of the Statute has not been made within five (5) working days reckoned from the date of notification made under paragraph 1 above, the Tribunal shall decide on the substance of the case.

SECTION V: Intervention, Third Parties, and Amicus Curiae

Rule 16

Intervention by Individuals

1.   Any person to whom the Tribunal is open under Article II, paragraph 2 of the Statute may apply to intervene at any stage prior to the listing of a case on the ground that he or she has a right which may be affected by the judgment to be given by the Tribunal. A person seeking to intervene shall file a request for intervention in the form of Annex II or its electronic equivalent in accordance with the conditions laid down in this Rule. The same shall apply to a request for intervention by the Chairperson of the Pension Committee if he or she considers that his or her administration may be affected by a judgment to be given by the Tribunal.

2.   The rules regarding the preparation and submission of applications shall apply *mutatis mutandis* to the request for intervention.

3.   The Tribunal shall rule on the admissibility of every request for intervention submitted under this rule.

4.   After ascertaining that the filing requirements of this rule have been complied with, the Executive Secretary shall provide a copy of the request for intervention to the Applicant and to the Bank. The President of the Tribunal shall decide which documents, if any, relating to the proceedings are to be provided to the potential intervenor by the Executive Secretary.

Rule 17

Third Parties; Amicus Curiae

1.   When it appears that a person may have an interest in the outcome of an application, the Tribunal, or when not in session, the President may instruct the Executive Secretary to provide a copy of the application submitted in the case and invite comments within a specified time. Any such comments shall be provided to the parties, who may submit their observations on the comments within the time specified. The Tribunal, or when not in session, the President shall then decide that the person should be invited to participate in the proceedings, and if the invitation is accepted, that person shall have the corresponding rights and obligations of a party.

2.   The Tribunal may permit any person or entity with a substantial interest in the outcome of a case to participate as a friend-of-the-court (*amicus curiae*). It may also permit the duly authorized representatives of the Staff Council of the Bank to participate.

SECTION VI: Provisional Measures; Consolidation

Rule 18

Provisional Measures

Within the limits of Article X, paragraph 5 of the Statute ("the filing of an application shall not have the effect of suspending execution of the decision contested"), the Tribunal or, if not in session, the President of the Tribunal may in exceptional cases, and for reasons stated, order provisional measures to be taken to permit proper adjudication of an application.

Rule 19

Consolidation

When considering that identical issues of fact or law are presented, the Tribunal or, when it is not in session the President may, on its own initiative or at the request of the Applicant, the Bank, or an intervenor, consolidate cases or any aspect of the proceedings in a case.

SECTION VII: Decisions, Judgments, and their Publication

Rule 20

Deliberations and Judgments

1.   The Tribunal shall deliberate in closed session. Deliberations of the Tribunal are confidential.

2.   At any time before rendering its judgment, the Tribunal may on its own motion provide for the confidentiality of any person mentioned in the case.

3.   Once a judgment has been adopted in accordance with Article IX of the Statute, it shall be signed by the President of the Tribunal, the members participating in the panel, and the Executive Secretary.

4.   The judgment in a case is final and binding.

Rule 21

Notification and Publication of Decisions/Judgments

1.   The Executive Secretary shall arrange for the publication of the final decisions and judgments of the Tribunal.

2.   The Executive Secretary shall provide each party with the final decision or judgment in a case prior to its publication.

SECTION VIII: Correction or Revision of a Decision/Judgment

Rule 22

Discovery of Clerical or Arithmetic Error

1.   The Tribunal may on its own initiative correct a clerical or arithmetic error in a final decision or judgment. It may also do so at the request of a party if filed within ninety (90) days of the party's receipt of the judgment. The parties may be invited to present their observations on such a correction.

Discovery of a Fact

2.   In accordance with Article XI of the Statute regarding discovery of a fact which (a) by its nature might have had a decisive influence on the judgment of the Tribunal, and (b) was unknown to both the party and the Tribunal at the time of delivery of the final decision or judgment, that party may request the Tribunal to revise it. Such a request must be filed within six (6) months after the party acquired knowledge of this fact, and in any case not later than five years from the date of the final decision or judgment.

3.   In either case, the request with its supporting documentation shall be notified to the other party, which shall have an opportunity to submit its observations.

SECTION IX: Miscellaneous Provisions

Rule 23

Modification and Supplementation of Rules

1.   The Tribunal or, when it is not in session, the President, after consulting the other members of the Tribunal, may:

   (a)   in exceptional cases, modify the application of these rules, including any time limits thereunder; and

   (b)   deal with any matter not expressly provided for in the present rules.

2.   The Tribunal may issue practice directions.

Rule 24

Code of Ethics

The Code of Ethics for Members of the Asian Development Bank Administrative Tribunal was adopted with effect from 28 February 2018. The Tribunal may amend, supplement, or replace it.

Rule 25

Entry into Force

The present rules shall apply to any application filed after 1 March 2021.

ANNEX I

A.   FORM OF FIRST SECTION OF APPLICATION AND REQUIREMENTS FOR ANNEXES UNDER RULE 6

Information concerning the personal and official status of the Applicant.

1.   Applicant:

   (a)   name and first names;

   (b)   date and place of birth;

   (c)   nationality; and

   (d)   telephone or cell phone number and postal and electronic addresses for purposes of the proceedings.

2.   Name, telephone or cell phone number, and postal and electronic addresses of person representing the Applicant before the Tribunal (if any).

3.   Official status of Applicant (see Statute, Article II):

    (a)   office/department where the Applicant works or worked at the time of the decision contested;

    (b)   effective date of contract;

    (c)   title and level at time of decision contested; and

    (d)   type of Applicant's appointment.

4.   If the Applicant was not a staff member at the time of the contested decision, state:

    (a)   the name, first names, nationality, and official status of the staff member whose rights are relied on; and

    (b)   the relation of the Applicant to the said staff member who entitles the former to come before the Tribunal.

5.   Date of the decision contested.

6.   Description of remedies exhausted within the Bank.

7.   The Applicant's request, if any, for anonymity, with reasons.

B.   REQUIREMENTS REGARDING ANNEXES

1.   Each document shall constitute a separate annex and shall be numbered with an Arabic numeral and certified. The word "ANNEX", followed by the number of the document, shall appear at the top of the first page.

2.   The annexed documents shall be preceded by a table of contents indicating the number, title, nature, date, and where appropriate, symbol of each annex.

3.   The words "see annex," followed by the appropriate number shall appear in parentheses after each reference to an annexed document in the other sections of the application.

4.   Whenever possible, annexes should be attached in chronological order.

ANNEX II

FORM OF FIRST SECTION OF REQUEST FOR INTERVENTION UNDER ARTICLE VI OF THE STATUTE AND RULE 16

Information concerning the personal and official status of the intervenor.

1.   Case in which intervention is sought.

2. Intervenor:

   (a) name and first names;

   (b) date and place of birth;

   (c) nationality; and

   (d) telephone or cell phone number, and postal and electronic addresses for purposes of the proceedings.

3. Name, telephone or cell phone number, and postal and electronic addresses of person representing the intervenor before the Tribunal.

4. Official status of intervenor:

   (a) office/department where the intervenor works or worked as staff member;

   (b) effective date of contract;

   (c) title and level; and

   (d) type of intervenor's appointment.

5. If the intervenor was not a staff member at the time of the contested decision, state:

   (a) the name, first names, nationality, and official status of the staff member whose rights are relied on; and

   (b) the title under which the intervenor claims he or she is entitled to the rights of the said staff member.

www.ingramcontent.com/pod-product-compliance
Lightning Source LLC
Chambersburg PA
CBHW042033220326
41599CB00045BA/7293